People of Destiny

A Humanities Series

There comes a time,
we know not when,
that marks
the destiny of men.

Joseph Addison Alexander

People of Destiny

LOUIS ARMSTRONG

By Kenneth G. Richards

For their cooperation in reviewing this manuscript, the editors wish to express their appreciation to Mr. Louis Armstrong and Mr. Joseph G. Glaser.

CHILDRENS PRESS, CHICAGO

The editors wish to express
their appreciation to Mr. Meyer Goldberg,
who created the series and inspired
the publication of People of Destiny.

Cover and body design: John Hollis

Project editor: Joan Downing

Editorial assistant: Gerri Stoller

Illustrations: Bob Brunton—Hollis
Associates

Research editor: Robert Hendrickson

Photographs: From the files of Wide World
Photos, Inc., Down Beat, George Hoefer,
Jack Bradley, Orrin Keepnews and Jane
Grauer, and Frederic Ramsey, Jr.

Typesetting: American Typesetting Co.

Printing: The Regensteiner Corporation

Words to the song "Basin Street Blues" used by permission of the
copyright owner, Mayfair Music Corp.
Quotations on pages 18; 19; 22, col. 2, ll. 14-22; 26; 29; 33; 35;
36; 37; 38; 39; 40; 43; 48; 55, col. 2; 56; 59; 63; 65; and 67 from
SATCHMO: My Life in New Orleans, by Louis Armstrong.
© 1954 by Louis Armstrong. Published by Prentice-Hall, Inc.,
Englewood Cliffs, New Jersey.
Quotations on pages 22, col. 2, ll. 6-8; 55, col. 1; 75; 78; and 79
from A History of Jazz in America, by Barry Ulanov. Published
by The Viking Press, Inc.
Quotation on page 88 from the January 22, 1959, issue of Down
Beat magazine.

Contents

Diplomat With a Horn

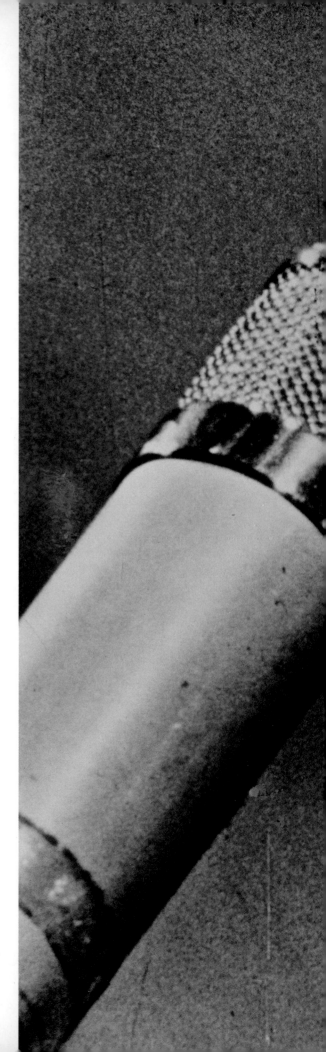

A capacity crowd packed the *Sport-palast* in West Berlin one night in February of 1959. They sat expectantly before the stage where Joseph Goebbels, Hitler's Minister of Propaganda, had once screamed the dogma of Nazi racial supremacy. Swastikas no longer festooned the walls and the echoes of *Sieg Heil!* had long since faded away. That night, Berliners had come to enjoy and pay homage to an American who played and sang a form of music that had been banned in the days of Adolf Hitler. Jazz was king in West Berlin and the greatest jazz player of them all was there to fill the air with sounds from New Orleans. Louis "Satchmo" Armstrong was in town.

The crowd was beginning to get restless when suddenly from behind the curtain came the soaring wail of a trumpet. The audience was instantly stilled, and as the curtains slowly parted to reveal the trumpeter and his six All Stars, the music was drowned in a rising crescendo of applause. "Louie! Louie!" the crowd screamed in a thunderous welcome that had barely subsided as the band finished its introductory number.

"Won't-cha come along wit' me
Down the Mis-sis-sip-pi?
We'll take the boat—to the lan' of dreams
Steamin' down the river, down to New Orleans."

The roly-poly figure in a tuxedo, moved forward to the microphone. A spotlight flashed, revealing the rolling eyes and wide smile that were familiar to people nearly everywhere in the world. Louis made a sweeping bow, with a handkerchief in one hand and a trumpet in the other, and then signaled the band to start the next number.

The piano tinkled an introduction. Bass and drums picked up the beat. Louis stepped closer to the microphone and the warm, gravelly, familiar voice filled the hall with lyrics he had been singing for forty years.

"Won't-cha come along wit' me
Down the Mis-sis-sip-pi?
We'll take the boat—to the lan' of dreams
Steamin' down the river, down to New Orleans."

New Orleans. It had been the "land of dreams" for Louis Armstrong. As a

boy in the area known as "Back O' Town," Louis had dreamed his dreams of making music—the deep, soulful music with which he shared a common birthplace. But his dreams were destined to carry him far from New Orleans —to Chicago, New York, Hollywood, and even to a crowded stadium in West Berlin.

"The band's there to greet us,
Old friends to meet us,
Where all the light and dark
folks meet—
Heaven on earth, they call it
Basin Street."

The journey from Basin Street—or, more exactly, Perdido Street—to Berlin had been a long one. Along the way there had been many disappointments, frustrations, and heartbreaks. But genius will not be denied and Louis Armstrong was a genius with the trumpet. At first, the music he loved and played was not

readily accepted beyond the close circle of enthusiasts who shared the emotions he expressed with his horn. But the warmth and beauty of his style, his exquisite tone and clarity, and his natural gifts as an entertainer, gradually broke down the barriers that surrounded the music called jazz. Even as he played that night in the *Sportpalast*, his powerful notes were hammering at yet another barrier.

In the audience that evening were an estimated 2000 Germans who had crossed over from East Berlin where communist doctrine officially frowned on jazz as a symbol of capitalist immorality. These were the days before the infamous Berlin Wall. The East Berliners had heard of jazz and their curiosity overcame the fear of censure or communist reprisals upon their return. They watched and listened as Louis and his All Stars spoke in eloquent tones the language of this purely American culture. And they surrendered to it.

It was a voice they could understand —speaking an international language that knew no shackles and recognized no Iron Curtain. As it had once expressed the emotions and raised the spirits of a restricted people in New Orleans, it now did the same for the East Berliners who lived under the heavy hand of communist repression. Soon their feet were tapping to the pounding rhythm and bouncing beat of

"Where all the light and dark folks meet—

Heaven on earth—they call it Basin Street."

American jazz. The notes and melodies Louis Armstrong made that night would be carried back to East Berlin. And as they were hummed and whistled later, by those who had come to the *Sportpalast*, they would echo all over East Germany. A trumpet player named Louis Armstrong was spreading the gospel of jazz.

> *"Basin Street is the street*
> *Where the elite always meet*
> *In New Orleans*
> *The lan' of dreams;*
> *You'll never know how nice it seems*
> *Or just how much it really means"*

Most of the audience could not understand the words of the famous "Basin Street Blues." But they could easily recognize the joy and love the song expressed as Louis, with eyes closed and body swaying, poured out the lyrics with all the vibrant warmth he felt within him.

> *"Glad to be—*
> *Yessirree—*
> *Where welcome's free,*
> *Dear to me,*
> *Where I can lose*
> *My Basin Street Blues!"*

For any other singer the song would be ended. But as the many Louis Armstrong fans in the *Sportpalast* knew, there was one more line. In the brief pause that followed, an international cooperative effort was silently agreed upon. As the band struck the final key, German voices joined with Louis' for the ending that has become an Armstrong trademark . . .

"OOOHHH YEEAAHHH!"

"OOOHHH YEEAAHHH!"

Twin Birth in New Orleans

Louis Armstrong and his music share a common birthplace—the crowded Negro district of New Orleans. No time can be set as the specific birthdate of jazz. This completely American art form evolved slowly and gradually over several decades. Like a giant oak, its roots extend in many directions, touching nearly every musical form. Jazz has been influenced by beats and rhythms and tones of music from around the world and of many centuries. It takes many shapes and forms. But whether the history of jazz is traced backward from the music of today or forward from the music of yesterday, the search leads through the Negro district of New Orleans.

It was in this district, too, that on July 4, 1900, Daniel Louis Armstrong was born. His birthplace was a steaming, fifty-cents-per-month room on the second floor of a dilapidated frame building in James Alley. There was no gas, electricity, or running water and the one room served as kitchen, dining room, bedroom, and living room. Outside, the alley was littered with discarded junk—broken furniture, battered pots and pans, parts of old wagons—the bric-a-brac of the slums. The only thing of beauty in the alley was a great old blue acacia tree, called the Chinaball tree by the local residents.

It was to this dreary environment that Louis' father, Willie Armstrong, had brought his bride, Mary Ann, in the year 1899. Willie was a tall, handsome young man. He had a job in a nearby turpentine factory—a job he was to hold until his death in 1933. Mayann, as Louis' mother was called, was born in Butte, Louisiana, and was only fifteen at the time of her marriage. The Arm-

strongs came to James Alley with little more than their love for one another and the hope of somehow, someday, moving to a more-desirable neighborhood.

Mayann worked for a New Orleans family, and at first the young couple got along well on their combined earnings. Then came the promise of a baby. With her characteristic strength and stubbornness, Mayann worked at her job until the very last. Finally, in the steaming, humid heat of a New Orleans summer, she delivered a strong, healthy baby boy. Even as Mayann nursed her tiny baby, the streets of New Orleans echoed to a new style of music in celebration of this first Independence Day of the twentieth century. It had a new beat, new tones, and a distinctive rhythm and style. As yet it had no name, but in future years, as it grew in popularity, people would call it "jazz."

The months rolled by and soon little Louis was toddling around the room. On nice days he played in the alley under the watchful eye of his grandmother. He, of course, did not recognize at this early age the poverty in which he lived. He was as well fed and clothed as the other little children in the alley. And he was showered with affection by his parents and his grandmother and even his great-grandmother, who had been born a slave.

But the poverty and squalor of the alley were beginning to tell on Willie and Mayann. Their long hours at work were resulting only in a bare existence at home. Their hopes of being able to move to a better area began to dwindle and the frustrations of their way of life began to shatter the foundations of their marriage. Shortly after the birth of Louis' sister, Beatrice, his father left

17

home and never came back. Louis was three years old.

Things did not change appreciably for the boy. His grandmother continued to care for him during the day while his mother worked. Thus, it was through his grandmother that Louis received his first training and guidance.

"She spent the best of her days raising me, and teaching me right from wrong," Louis remembers. "Whenever I did something she thought I ought to get a whipping for, she sent me out to get a switch from the big old Chinaball tree. With tears in my eyes I would go to the tree and return with the smallest switch I could find. Generally she would laugh and let me off. However, when she was really angry she would give me a whipping for everything wrong I had done for weeks."

Another year went by, and Louis was now almost five years old. Amid the trash and discarded furniture of the alley, Louis and his pals scrambled around in their bare feet playing pirates or cowboys, tag or hide-and-seek. For a happy-go-lucky five-year-old it was a wonderful life. The steady diet of stale bread and red beans or rice didn't bother him a bit. He was a robust child, rarely sick, and the little wounds of childhood were nearly always healed with old-fashioned home-prepared remedies.

The only thing of beauty in James Alley, the street in the Negro district of New Orleans where Louis Armstrong was born, was a great old blue acacia tree (above), called the Chinaball tree by the local residents. Louis' grandmother cared for him while his mother worked, and he remembers that "whenever I did something she thought I ought to get a whipping for, she sent me out to get a switch from the big old Chinaball tree. With tears in my eyes I would go to the tree and return with the smallest switch I could find."

In later years, Louis remembered his mother's remedy for an infected foot or toe. "Mother and some of her neighbors would go to the railroad tracks and fill baskets with pepper grass. She would boil this until it got real gummy and rub it on the wound. Then within two or three hours we kids would get out of bed and be playing around the streets as though nothing had happened."

Mayann finally decided she had to move away from James Alley. Louis was now reaching an age when the sordid environment would begin to exert its influence on him.

Late in the summer of 1905, Mayann and her two children moved some eighteen blocks away to a one-room flat on the corner of Liberty and Perdido Streets. The room itself was little better than the one in James Alley had been, but the squalid atmosphere of the alley had been left behind. Mayann felt better about Louis and his sister growing up in the busy and bustling scene of which they were now a part.

For young Louis, though, it was a time of trial. It had been difficult to leave his old friends and playmates behind and it was even more difficult to be accepted by the established gang in his new location. Each new boy had to "prove" himself before being accepted, and Louis was no exception.

Despite the environment of James Alley, Mayann had always kept Louis neatly dressed and his grandmother had taught him to be polite and respectful of others. Consequently, to the gang at the corner of Liberty and Perdido Streets, Louis seemed to be something of a "mama's boy." But, despite his quiet way and neat appearance, Louis was anything but a sissy. The boys in the gang on the corner were not long in discovering this.

On his first day in the new neighborhood, Louis ran into a group who immediately decided to test him. They crowded around Louis and the biggest and toughest member of the group called him some names and then picked up some mud and threw it on his clean suit. The others barely had time to guffaw at the plight of their target when Louis exploded into a veritable whirlwind. As frightened as he was, the thought of his soiled clothes so infuriated Louis that he smashed the bully square in the mouth and nose with all his might. Taken by surprise at the fury of Louis' assault, the bully retreated before the onslaught and his pals decided that discretion was the better part of valor. With blood streaming from his injured nose and lips, the gang leader and his cronies raced off—leaving Louis too surprised to follow. The next time

19

When Louis was about eight years old, he began selling newspapers after school along St. Charles Street, a street much like the one shown at left. During his hours of selling papers, he had his first contact with the music of New Orleans. In those days there were honky-tonk saloons on nearly every corner, each with its own little band that featured all the varied music forms of the era, from blues to ragtime.

they met, Louis was accepted as one of the "gang." After that, no one wanted to start trouble with the boy from James Alley.

That fall, Louis began attending Fisk School, just a block from his home. He was an average student and was very popular with the other children. A quiet and ambitious youngster, he was always anxious to please and to make friends. He grew to love the area around Liberty and Perdido Streets and during the occasional periods when he was sent to live with his grandmother for a few weeks, he missed his friends and the haunts he now knew so well.

Mayann was working as a cook for a wealthy family on the other side of town. Some nights Louis would make the long walk over there. Inside the kitchen, which seemed of regal splendor to the wide-eyed Louis, Mayann would feed him. On some occasions, she would let the boy follow her upstairs where he would marvel at the lovely furnishings.

About 1907 or 1908, Louis began selling papers along St. Charles Street. Soon after school was out, he would pick up his papers, tuck them under his arm and move along the street shouting "*States* or *Item! States* or *Item!*" Sometimes he would call out the headlines of the day. "Taft Elected President!" or "Former President Cleveland Dies!" Finally, when all the papers were sold, Louis would walk wearily home and turn his meager earnings over to his mother or grandmother. After a late dinner of red beans he would fall into bed and sleep soundly until morning when it was time to get up and be off to school once more.

It was during his hours of selling papers along the streets that young Louis had his first contact with the music of New Orleans. In those days there were honky-tonk saloons on nearly every corner. The most famous of them all was the Funky Butt Hall, near Louis' home. Each honky-tonk had its own little band that featured all the varied music forms of the era, from blues to ragtime. Buddy Bolden, one of the first jazz players, frequently played at the Funky Butt. Bolden's music was the boy's first introduction to the sound Louis was destined to master in the years to come.

Children, of course, were not allowed in the hall. The building, however, was a dilapidated edifice with huge cracks in the walls. Louis and his pals would sneak around the sides of the hall, watch the dancers through the cracks, and clap their hands to the dynamic new rhythms of Buddy Bolden. Sometimes, caught up in the frantic beat, the children would stage their own impromptu dancing on the sidewalk as the music reverberated in the old building and echoed along the streets.

Bolden was a cornetist who worked himself into a frenzy as he blew his horn louder and harder than anyone. He was a dynamic entertainer who would parade his band through the streets prior to an evening performance, drumming up business like a Pied Piper. Louis and his pals would distribute handbills advertising Buddy Bolden's performances at Funky Butt Hall. By dance time, the hall would be filled to capacity. Then Buddy would blow his horn in frantic tempo until the wee hours of the morning. Eventually, Bolden was committed to a mental institution. The people on Perdido Street say he blew too hard and too long. But

Buddy Bolden had set a precedent in jazz that would remain and influence the New Orleans styling for years to come. Barry Ulanov, in his great book *A History of Jazz in America*, writes: "Buddy Bolden's band set the instruments and perhaps the harmonic and melodic order (of jazz) as well."

In later years Louis would remember his impressions of the early greats of jazz who were playing at the Funky Butt Hall when he was a boy. At a very early age, Louis developed an interest in the cornet and trumpet. "There was something about the instrument that caught my ears," he said.

"All in all Buddy Bolden was a great musician, but I think he blew too hard," Louis wrote later. "The king of all the musicians was Joe Oliver, the finest trumpeter who ever played in New Orleans."

This same Joe "King" Oliver was to become the greatest single influence on the musical career of his young admirer. A close and warm relationship would develop between the two as Louis got older. And though he could never have dreamed it then, in the years to come there would be many who would differ with Louis' evaluation of New Orleans trumpeters.

Countless thousands of jazz enthusiasts today will tell you that the greatest trumpeter ever to come out of New Orleans is a fellow called "Satchmo."

The most famous of the New Orleans honky-tonks was Funky Butt Hall, near Louis' home. Children were not allowed inside, but Louis and his friends would sneak around the sides of the hall, watch the dancers through the cracks in the wall, and clap their hands to the dynamic new rhythms of the early greats of jazz who played there. At a very early age, Louis developed an interest in the cornet and trumpet. "There was something about the instrument that caught my ears," he said. The trumpeter he most admired was Joe "King" Oliver, who was to become the greatest single influence on the musical career of young Louis. A close and warm relationship would develop between the two as Louis got older.

"...The king of all the musicians was Joe Oliver, the finest trumpeter who ever played in New Orleans."

The "Second Liner"

Louis loved music and in the Negro district of New Orleans there was much music to be heard. Besides the nightly refrains that blared forth from the honky-tonks, there were the church spirituals sung at prayer meetings and Sunday services; the songs of the men who worked along the levees of the Mississippi; the work songs that found their way into New Orleans from the cotton fields of the South; and the songs of the railroad workers with their musical sagas of legendary railroad men like *John Henry*.

But the music most often heard by young Louis was that of the marching Negro bands. Louis knew many men who were bartenders, barbers, or janitors by trade, but who were musicians in their spare time—generally for little more than the sheer enjoyment of playing. And it seemed as if there were always bands marching somewhere for one reason or another. They marched for political rallies or weddings or to publicize coming events such as prizefights or picnics. Wherever they marched, the bands were sure to be closely fol-

There was much music to be heard in the Negro district of New Orleans, but the music most often heard by young Louis was that of the marching Negro bands that played for political rallies, weddings and funerals, or to publicize coming events such as prizefights or picnics. Wherever they marched, the bands were sure to be closely followed by Louis and his pals, who kept perfect step as they strutted proudly, "second lining" behind the band.

In 1909, when he was nine years old, Louis quit school. He lied about his age to get a job delivering coal from a coal wagon. His job was to ride along on the wagon and deliver little buckets of coal to the women who called from their doors and windows. As the driver steered the mule slowly along the streets, Louis would call "Stone coal, ladies, five cents a water bucket!" When a housewife called back, Louis would hop down from the wagon and race up the stairs with a bucket of coal. Sometimes he would be asked to light the fire, a job that usually meant a small tip for the hard-working youngster. Each night, Louis would bring home to his mother the seventy-five cents or dollar he had made that day.

lowed by Louis and his pals, who kept perfect step as they strutted proudly, "second lining" behind the band.

Sometimes a whole band would be lifted into huge horse-drawn furniture wagons. Whenever two such groups chanced to meet they would stage a contest to see who could outplay the other. While the two bands blasted the air with ragtime, Louis and his friends danced around the wagons until they were exhausted.

The bands frequently marched at funerals. Following the hearse on the trip to the cemetery, a band would play such hymns as "Rock of Ages" and "Nearer, My God, to Thee." With the body at last laid to rest, the band would change its music for the return trip. The expression "goin' to town" stems from these trips back from the graveyard. The mood changed as the procession left the cemetery. The step livened and spirits soared as the bandsmen filled the air with the musical question, "Didn't He Ramble?" The sadness of the occasion was soon forgotten as children danced gaily to the blasting notes of "High Society" and "King Porter Stomp" or "Maple Leaf Rag."

In his autobiography, Louis described a typical procession returning from the cemetery. "Once the band starts, everybody starts swaying from one side of the street to the other, especially those who drop in and follow the ones who have been to the funeral. These people are known as the 'second line' and they may be anyone passing along the street who wants to hear the music. The spirit hits them and they follow along to see what's happening. Some follow only a few blocks, but others follow the band until the whole affair is over."

There was music everywhere along the streets and alleys and squares of New Orleans.

In 1909, when he was nine years old, Louis quit school. He lied about his age to get a job delivering coal from a coal wagon. His job was to ride along on the wagon and deliver little buckets of coal to the women who called from their doors and windows.

"Stone coal, ladies, five cents a water bucket! Stone coal, five cents a bucket!" Louis would call as the driver steered the mule slowly along the streets.

When a housewife called back, Louis would hop down from the wagon and race up the stairs with a bucket of coal. Sometimes a lady would ask him to light the fire, a job that usually meant a small tip for the hard-working youngster.

The delivery made, Louis would jump back on the wagon and refill the bucket as the wagon rolled slowly on to the next stop. Each night he would bring home to his mother, who was now remarried, the seventy-five cents or dollar he had made that day.

On his rounds, Louis noticed several groups of boys who sang and danced on street corners for the amusement of passersby. Louis was amused, too, by the delightful antics of these children his own age, but he became especially interested when he noticed that their audience was often generous when the boys passed the hat after each performance. Why couldn't he and his pals do something like that?

One night Louis talked it over with three of his chums—Little Mack, Big Nose Sidney, and Redhead Happy. They sang and danced together for their own enjoyment—perhaps they could put an act together and make some spending money.

His pals were enthusiastic. "That's a great idea, Dipper," one of them said. "Let's get started!"

"Dipper" was short for "Dippermouth"—a nickname given Louis when he was very young. Later, someone changed it to "Satchelmouth," which in turn was shortened to "Satchmo"—a name that was destined to become famous in the world of jazz.

Louis knew that an "act" would require preparation and rehearsals, so the boys began testing ideas and working out "routines" that very night. For a couple of weeks they met after supper each evening in a deserted yard and went over their repertoire of songs and dances. At last they felt they were ready for their big entry into "show business."

In the spring of 1912, the boys often made their way down Rampart Street, singing their song routines as they went. Whenever anyone stopped to listen, the boys went into their act. They would begin with a ragtime tune like "Jack Carey," which was later to become "Tiger Rag." Then, singing in harmony, they would switch to a traditional refrain like "Swanee River." Little Mack sang the lead while Redhead Happy and Big Nose Sidney sang bass and baritone. Louis sang a rich, high tenor. To his countless millions of later-day fans, it seems amazing that Louis Armstrong was ever a tenor. But the hoarse, throaty voice of later years had not yet developed in the Satchmo of 1912.

While they set the beat with clapping hands and tapping feet, Louis would

sometimes carry the lead on such songs as "My Brazilian Beauty" or "Mr. Moon Won't You Please Shine Down On Me?" Between songs they would put on little skits, and when their last song ended, Little Mack would do a series of somersaults as a grand finale. They would then bow to their audience, who showered them with pennies. The little group would scurry around picking up the offerings and then move farther along the street to attract a new audience. Later, as they headed for home, they divided their earnings equally. On good nights, each would have a dollar or more to carry home.

The enterprise was a great success for several months, especially on holiday nights such as Carnival Night or Fourth of July, when the crowds were in a gay, festive mood. With this in mind, the boys looked forward eagerly to New Year's Eve of 1912. There would be large, happy crowds out on that evening, waiting to ring in the new year of 1913. Louis and the boys were sure it would be a record night for their enterprise.

New Year's Eve in New Orleans was always a noisy and jubilant celebration, complete with torchlight parades and fireworks. Louis and his pals had no fireworks, but in the bottom of his mother's old trunk Louis had found a .38-caliber pistol loaded with blank ammunition. Deciding this would make an excellent noisemaker, he sneaked the gun out without his mother's knowledge.

As he and his singing companions strolled along Rampart Street, a boy on the other side of the street suddenly began firing a little pistol, also loaded with blanks. The quartet all laughed and one of the boys goaded Louis with: "Go get him Dipper."

Louis' gun made a louder noise than the other boy's did, and Louis fired all six shots at the frightened youngster, who "cut out like a jackrabbit."

But Louis had no more than fired his last cartridge when he felt strong arms encircle him from behind and the gun being grabbed out of his hand. Turning to see who his assailant was, Louis looked directly into the eyes of a tall, stern detective. As the other boys raced off in different directions, Louis pleaded with the man not to arrest him.

But the strong arms were unrelenting and the sobbing, frightened Louis found himself carried off to Juvenile Court. By ten o'clock that evening, he was locked in a cell. Louis cried himself to sleep.

For a twelve-year-old boy, a jail cell seemed like the end of the world. But this, the saddest night he had ever known, was to mark a turning point in the life of Louis Armstrong.

New Year's Eve, 1912, was to mark a turning point in the life of Louis Armstrong. He and his friends had looked forward to the night of jubilant celebration, which in New Orleans was always complete with torchlight parades and fireworks. The boys had no fireworks to set off, but in the bottom of his mother's old trunk, Louis found a pistol loaded with blank ammunition. When the long-awaited night came, and Louis fired his illegal noisemaker, he was immediately picked up by a police detective and taken to Juvenile Court. By ten o'clock that evening, he was locked in a cell, where he cried himself to sleep. Though the jail cell seemed like the end of the world to the twelve-year-old boy, it was from here that he was sent to the Colored Waifs' Home for Boys and a whole new start in life.

The Musical Waif

The first day of the New Year, 1913, dawned through a dripping gray sky. Louis, still weary from having cried himself to sleep, awoke in the bare, cold cell. The gray light slanting through the window added to his fear and apprehension.

"What's to become of me?" he wondered fearfully. "Will they tell my mother where I am? Will Mayann come and get me out of here?"

Oh! how he prayed that Mayann or his stepfather or grandmother—or any friendly person—would appear at the door, gather him up, and take him home. But even as he prayed, a figure did appear in the doorway—that of a giant policeman.

"Come on kid, we have to be going," the man said.

Louis followed quietly as the policeman led him out of the building into the yard where a police van was waiting.

"Go on, get in," said the policeman holding open the door at the back of the wagon. Louis climbed in quietly to find several other boys who had been picked up the night before already seated inside. None knew where they were being taken, but now that he was not alone, Louis felt a little of the fear leave him.

Presently the wagon began to move. Louis and the other boys sat quietly as they rolled and swayed along the damp city streets. Louis was unable to tell where they were going. He had prayed that he was being taken back to Perdido Street, but as the ride continued longer and longer, he knew his hopes were in vain.

At last the wagon stopped. When the door opened, the policeman motioned for the boys to step down. The drizzle had stopped and Louis squinted his eyes as he stepped out into the sunlight. Looking around for something or someone he could recognize, he was amazed to find that they were on the outskirts of the city. Across the way was a big dairy farm where dozens of cows, calves, and horses were grazing or prancing around in the fields. Nearby, honeysuckle trees wafted their fragrance into the morning air. For Louis, the unfamiliar scene was breathtaking. For a

When he first arrived at the Waif's Home on New Year's Day, 1913, Louis was homesick, frightened, and miserable. He wrote a postcard to his mother, Mayann (opposite, sitting), and his sister, who was called Mama Lucy (opposite, standing) begging them to come and take him home.

Though Louis went through days of loneliness and despair during his first weeks at the Waifs' Home, he soon became very popular with the other boys and learned how to do many indoor and outdoor chores (right). The boys also learned discipline. Many, like Louis, for the first time. There was no more roaming the streets selling newspapers or entertaining passersby. There was no more listening to the music of the Funky Butt Hall or other honky-tonks in the Third Ward. "Lights out" came at nine o'clock. "The place was more like a health center or a boarding school than a boys' jail," Louis remembers. "We played all kinds of sports, and we turned out some mighty fine baseball players, swimmers, and musicians. All in all I am proud of the days I spent at the Colored Waifs' Home for Boys."

moment he forgot his fears as he took in the sights, sounds, and smells of his first visit beyond the city's streets and alleys.

But he was soon reminded of his predicament as he and the other boys were herded toward a rather drab and sprawling building that bore a sign identifying it as the "Colored Waifs' Home for Boys." At the entrance to the home they were met by the superintendent, Mr. Jones, and his wife—a stern but not unpleasant couple who bid the boys welcome. Also standing in the entrance was Mr. Davis, who was identified as the head warden. As the boys were ushered into the building, the wagon pulled away and Louis' old fears returned once more.

The boys were given uniforms to wear and were registered as "transients." They were told that in a few days they would be taken once more to Juvenile Court for a hearing before Judge Wilson. That afternoon, Louis wrote a postcard to Mayann and his sister Beatrice —who was now called Mama Lucy— begging them to come and take him home.

A week passed—days of loneliness and despair for the homesick Louis. At first he refused to eat, though he had to go to the dinner table with the other boys. No one tried to force him to eat and as dishes of food were passed his way, "I only pushed them away," Louis remembers. "I did the same thing for several days. The keepers, Mr. and Mrs. Jones and Mr. Alexander and Mr. Peter Davis, saw me refuse these meals, but they did not say anything about it. But on the fourth day I was so hungry I was first at the table."

Mayann and Mama Lucy at last came to see him and the little family had a tearful reunion in the home's reception room. Louis tried to be brave and assured them that he was being treated well and that the food was good. There was nothing they could do for the boy until he had his hearing at Juvenile Court.

A few days later, Louis appeared before Judge Wilson. Mayann came to court to testify that Louis was really a good boy and had never caused any serious trouble before. She knew he had meant to do no harm and was sure Louis

had learned his lesson and would never do it again. But Judge Wilson banged the gavel on his desk and announced that he was giving Louis an "indeterminate sentence." This meant that he would have to stay in the home until the superintendent decided he had mended his ways. Once more Louis bid his family a tearful good-bye and climbed into the police van for the long ride to his new home.

Louis, who made friends easily, was immediately popular with the other boys in the school. At the slightest request he would sing or dance or pantomime for the entertainment of those around him. His activities disrupted the routine of the school, however, and he was soon in trouble with Mr. Davis. "He gave me fifteen hard lashes on the hand," Louis remembers. "After that I was really scared of him for a long time."

Besides the basic grade-school subjects, the school offered vocational courses. As Louis recalls it, "Mr. Alexander taught the boys how to do carpentry, how to garden, and how to build campfires. Mr. Davis taught music and vocational training. Each boy had the right to choose the vocation which interested him.

"Quite naturally, I would make a beeline to Mr. Davis and his music. Music has been in my blood from the day I was born. When the orchestra practiced with Mr. Davis, who was a good teacher, I listened very carefully, but I did not dare go near the band though I wanted to in the worst way. I was afraid Mr. Davis would bawl me out or give me a few more lashes."

The privilege of playing in the home's brass band was granted only to those boys who showed good conduct and exemplary behavior. Louis ached to become a part of the brass band, and he soon recognized that he would have to impress Mr. Davis with good behavior if he was to realize his ambition. "I was beginning to adapt myself to the place, and since I had to stay there for a long time I thought I might as well adjust myself. I did."

Mr. Davis was aware of Louis' natural inclination to music and rhythm. He was also aware that the boy badly wanted to join the brass band and was striving his mightiest to earn the privilege. One evening as Louis was leaving the supper table, Mr. Davis put his hand on the boy's shoulder and asked, "Louis Armstrong, how would you like to join our brass band?" He might as well have asked a fish if he would like to swim or a bird if he'd like to fly. Even though he had been dreaming of just such a possibility for weeks, Louis remembers, "I was so speechless and so surprised I just could not answer him right away." The music teacher asked the question again and by this time Louis had caught his breath and blurted his reply. "Yessir, Mr. Davis, I certainly would!"

Visions of how he would look in his bandsman's uniform flashed through Louis' mind. "I had never tried to play the cornet, but while listening to the band every day I remembered Joe Oliver, Buddy Bolden, and Bunk Johnson. And I had an awful urge to learn the cornet."

Louis never considered the fact that Mr. Davis would give him any other instrument to play than the cornet. "I already pictured myself playing with all the power and endurance of Bunk, Joe, or Bolden," he remembers. Racing over to the music hall for rehearsal, he approached Mr. Davis full of hope and expectation.

"To my surprise," Louis recalls, "he handed me a tambourine, the little thing you tap with your fingers like a miniature drum. So that was the end of my beautiful dream!"

Louis accepted the disappointment philosophically and tried not to let his disillusionment show. He immediately set to work playing the little instrument to the best of his ability. The "music in

---

Louis ached to become a part of the Waifs' Home Brass Band, and finally the music teacher, Mr. Davis, asked him to join. Louis was overjoyed, even though his first instrument was a tambourine. He was a natural musician, however, and rapidly advanced to the drums, the alto, and the bugle. Louis (arrow) is shown with the band at right.

his blood" made him a natural musician and with his inborn sense of rhythm he had soon mastered the tambourine.

A few weeks later, the band's drummer left the home and Mr. Davis decided to give Louis the chance to fill the vacancy. Once again, Louis proved an eager and talented student. Just a few days after he took over the drums, the band was scheduled to play a concert. Mr. Davis wasn't sure that Louis could handle the drum "breaks"—or solos—involved in a particular piece called "At the Animals' Ball." Louis assured the teacher he could, and immediately began to learn the complicated triple-break routine that had taken the previous drummer many weeks to master.

On the day of the concert, Louis tried not to show the tension he was feeling as the time approached for the band to play "At the Animals' Ball." He played with an intense seriousness as he waited for the critical moment to arrive. At last the cue from Mr. Davis came, and Louis met the challenge with a masterly performance. With a smooth and powerful beat, he rolled through the triple break without a falter. Mr. Davis nodded his approval with a warm glance and when the concert ended, the other players clapped Louis on the back. Louis Armstrong, the bandsman, was tasting his first public acclaim for a musical performance.

Spring came early that year in New Orleans. Soon the buds were on the trees, and the lawns and shrubs of the Waifs' Home turned green and fragrant. Louis, busy with his studies and his band rehearsals, had little time to be homesick for Mayann and his pals on Perdido Street. There were also many chores to keep the boys busy.

"The Waifs' Home was surely a very clean place," Louis recalls, "and we did all the work ourselves. That's where I learned how to scrub floors, wash and

iron, cook, make up the beds, do a little of everything around the house."

The boys of the home also were learning discipline—many, like Louis, for the first time. There was no more roaming the streets selling papers or entertaining passersby. There was no more listening to the music of the Funky Butt Hall or other honky-tonks back in the Third Ward. At the home, "lights out" came in the dormitory at nine o'clock and all the boys were expected to be quiet and go to sleep.

"The place was more like a health center or a boarding school than a boy's jail," Louis remembers. "We played all kinds of sports, and we turned out some mighty fine baseball players, swimmers, and musicians. All in all I am proud of the days I spent at the Colored Waifs' Home for Boys."

The year 1913 was a memorable year in the United States. Two amendments to the Constitution were ratified—the sixteenth, which authorized the levying of income taxes by Congress, and the seventeenth, which provided for the popular election of United States Senators. It was also the year in which mass production came into being at the Ford plant in Detroit. Woodrow Wilson took the oath of office as twenty-eighth President of the United States and immediately broke a 113-year presidential precedent by appearing in person before a joint session of Congress. No president had done so since the days of John Adams in the year 1880.

For Louis Armstrong, now approaching his thirteenth birthday, this all had little meaning. He was wrapped up in his life at the home. But it was here, in this sprawling old building, that another memorable event was to take place in this summer of 1913. The exact date is not recorded, but on a warm summer evening Louis "Satchmo" Armstrong first put his lips to a cornet.

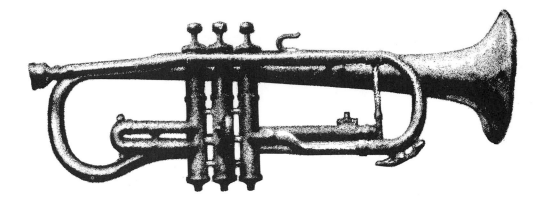

The First Horn

Louis Armstrong's switch from percussion instruments to wind instruments came early in the summer of 1913. He had progressed very well on the drums, and though his heroes were trumpeters Bolden, Oliver, and Johnson, he was delighted just to be a part of the band. His inborn bent for music made him a natural and talented performer on any instrument.

Mr. Davis was quick to recognize the latent musical talent of his young student. He watched with satisfaction as Louis applied himself diligently to his musical studies. One of the aims of the Waifs' Home was to find each boy's interest and assist in developing it into a suitable vocation. It was soon evident that there was nothing in this world that captured the interest of Louis Armstrong as much as music did. Mr. Davis decided to develop Louis' musical talent a step further.

One day Louis was called to the music hall where Mr. Davis met him with a question.

"You are doing very well on the drums, Louis," he said, "but I need an alto player. How about trying your luck?"

Louis was eager and full of confidence. "Anything you like, Mr. Davis."

With that, Mr. Davis handed Louis his first wind instrument, the little three-valved alto horn that is commonly called an "alto."

"I had been singing for a number of years and my instinct told me that an

Louis' dream was finally realized when Mr. Davis asked him if he would like to learn to play the cornet. It didn't take Louis long to decide. "I was in seventh heaven," he recalled later. And so began the love affair between Louis and his horn that was destined to make history in the decades to come.

alto takes a part in a band the same as a baritone or tenor in a quartet," Louis wrote later. "I played my part on the alto very well."

Within a very short time Louis was playing the alto as if he had been doing it for years. Mr. Davis watched and listened with pleasure and satisfaction as Louis demonstrated unusual power and lovely, true tones with his new instrument. By now the music teacher was convinced he had a child prodigy in his band.

Weeks passed and one day the home's bugler was released to his parents. This presented a rather critical problem because the home was run in a military fashion.

"Our life was regulated by bugle calls," Louis remembers. "A kid blew a bugle for us to get up, to go to bed, and to come to meals. The last call was the favorite with us all. Whether they were cutting trees a mile away or building a fire under the great kettle in the yard to scald our dirty clothes, the boys would hotfoot it back to the home when they heard the mess call. I envied the bugler because he had more chances to use his instrument than anyone else."

Someone had to be found right away to take the place of the departing boy. Mr. Davis immediately thought of Louis.

And so, for the fourth time in as many months, Louis was given a new instrument to master. And again Louis was up to the challenge. "I felt real proud of my position as bugler," he remembers. The first thing he did was to turn the tarnished and battered old horn into a gleaming instrument he could be proud of. All the boys agreed that it was a little easier to get out of bed in the morning to the full and beautiful tones that Louis blew on his bugle.

As the summer days became warm and lovely, the band was frequently called upon to play concerts or to march in parades. Louis loved the parades and was very proud to be strutting along to the blaring notes of a military march. It was along the march routes that the boys seemed to perform their best. With the crowds of spectators lining the streets and avenues cheering and applauding their exuberant efforts, the boys in the little band felt they could march forever. Of course, it was also wonderful to be beyond the confines of the home and back once more amid the teeming and bustling streets of New Orleans. "We were so glad to get a chance to walk in the street that we did not care how long we paraded or how far," Louis wrote later.

Then one day, Louis was introduced to the instrument that was to carry him to world fame in the realm of American jazz. Once more Mr. Davis came to Louis. "You have done well with other instruments, Louis," he said. "I would like you to learn to play the cornet. Would you like to try?"

Of course, it didn't take Louis long to decide. "I was in seventh heaven," he recalled later. "Unless I was dreaming, my ambition had been realized." He took the horn Mr. Davis handed him and kissed it in the simple gesture that he often repeats on stage to this day. And so began the love affair between Louis and his horn that was destined to make history in the decades to come.

Louis immediately began to spend all his spare time practicing on his cornet. He would sit by the hour developing his power and smoothing out his tones and high notes. He soon found that he had great difficulty keeping the mouthpiece at his lips. At last he arrived at a solution. Borrowing a file from the workshop tool keeper, he reshaped the mouthpiece to fit his lips. With his now-comfortable instrument, Louis rapidly developed into the finest cornetist the home had ever seen.

Mr. Davis was a traditionalist when it came to music. It should be played, he insisted, "as it was written." Consequently, he was angry whenever he found Louis taking the same kind of liberties with old favorites that Bolden and Oliver had taken back on Perdido Street. But despite Louis' occasional moments of weakness when he tried to "jazz up" a tune, Mr. Davis took immense pride in the performance of his star pupil. By the end of the summer, when it was evident that Louis was the master musician of the group, Mr. Davis made him the leader of the band.

For the thirteen-year-old cornet player, it was the thrill of his life. Years later he would recall the uniforms the boys wore so proudly. "The band's uniform consisted of long white pants turned up to look like knickers, black easy-walkers, or sneakers as they are now called, thin blue gabardine coats, black stockings, and caps with black and white bands. . . . To stand out as the leader of the band, I wore cream-colored pants, brown stockings, brown easy-walkers, and a cream-colored cap."

Then came the day Louis had often dreamed of. One Sunday the band was marching in the city, and Mr. Davis swung them out in the direction of Louis' old neighborhood. As they came nearer and nearer to the old haunts Louis knew so well, his heart began to pound. And then Mr. Davis turned the band up Perdido Street.

Almost immediately, the word spread like wildfire that Mayann's boy and his band were marching through the neighborhood. "Dipper's comin' with his band!"

As they neared Liberty Street, Louis was strutting as he had never strutted before. He recognized faces in the crowd that gathered quickly along the sidewalks. Redhead Happy and Big Nose Sidney were there. "There's Dipper!" they yelled. "Hey Dipper!"

As the band reached the intersection near Louis' home, he spotted Mayann and Mama Lucy standing on the corner. Both were beaming with pride as tears of joy streamed down their cheeks. Louis flashed them a broad grin as he strutted past, though he was very close to tears himself.

Mr. Davis brought the band to a halt in front of the Fisk School and told the band to "fall out" for a rest. Louis was immediately besieged by old friends and well-wishers. Mayann and Mama Lucy rushed up to him for a tearful and joyous reunion, and for a little while Louis was just about the proudest and happiest boy in New Orleans. He would savor these moments during all the rest of his stay at the Waifs' Home.

Winter came once more to New Orleans and with it the end of Louis' first year at the home. The sounds of fireworks and gaiety, echoing out from the city as people celebrated the New Year of 1914, reminded Louis of that fateful night just one year before. He lay on his bed in the dormitory considering the past twelve months and what they had meant to him. He still felt a certain homesickness, though Mayann and Mama Lucy visited him frequently. But life in the home wasn't bad, he decided. He had made many good friends and the people who ran the home liked him and treated him well. He also reminded himself that if he hadn't come to the home, perhaps he never would have had the chance to learn to play his treasured cornet. He finally nodded off to sleep as the last fireworks sputtered out in the streets of the city.

The months rolled by. Spring came and went, followed by the long hot days of summer. Across the sea, in Europe, there were rumors of war. In Mexico, American forces had bombarded and then occupied the coastal town of Veracruz and war was narrowly averted. But all this was little cause for concern to a boy, not yet fourteen, who asked only to be allowed to play his cornet. But Louis' days with the Waifs' Brass Band were destined to come to a close.

Louis' days with the Brass Band were destined to come to a close. His father gained the boy's release from the home in June, 1914. It was a tearful Louis who said his good-byes before he and his father, Willie, walked out to catch a streetcar into town (above).

Mayann urged Louis' father, who was now remarried, to go to the authorities and gain Louis' release from the home. Willie agreed to take Louis into his home and assume responsibility for the boy.

All the reports submitted by the home's superintendent and his staff indicated that Louis had been a model inmate with exemplary conduct. Although Mr. Davis hated to lose his finest musician, he felt that the boy should be allowed to go home. At last the case was brought once more to Juvenile Court and on June 16, 1914, Louis was released to the care of his father.

It was a tearful Louis who said his good-byes to all his friends and teachers on that hot summer day. The band played a few numbers and Louis joined them just to show his father how well he had progressed as a musician. Then, fighting back the tears, Louis handed his cornet back to Mr. Davis, who offered some kind words of encouragement.

"You've been a good boy, Louis," he said. "You have some very fine musical talent and I hope you'll continue to develop it. Keep up the good work."

At last Louis and his father walked out to City Park Avenue and caught a streetcar into town. Louis was quiet and subdued as the car rocked along the tracks to Poydras Street, where his father lived. Was this to be the end of his musical career? He owned no instrument and couldn't afford to buy one. A chapter had ended in his life and a new one was about to open. But even in his wildest dreams, young Louis Armstrong could not have imagined where his destiny was to lead him in the years to come.

Return to Perdido

Willie's wife, Gertrude, welcomed her stepson into their poor little home and Louis immediately became a part of the family. Willie and Gertrude had children of their own—two boys named Henry and Willie. This was Louis' first meeting with his stepbrothers. He immediately liked the younger boy, Henry, and they became good friends. Willie, Jr. was more difficult to get along with, however, and there were times when Louis, "wanted to throw a whole pot of beans at his head." Nonetheless, the little family got on well together, though Louis often missed the boys and teachers at the Waifs' Home. Gertrude, Louis would remember, "turned out to be a very fine woman, and she treated me just as though I were her own child. For that alone I will always love her."

While Willie and Gertrude worked each day, Louis was left to manage the household. The training and discipline he had received at the Waifs' Home served him well as Louis swept the floors, made the beds, and cooked for his stepbrothers while his parents were away. He would recall later that his biggest problem was getting something to eat for himself at mealtime.

"Whenever I cooked a big pot of beans and rice and ham hocks those boys would manage to eat up most of it before I could get to the table. Willie could make a plate of food vanish faster than anyone I ever saw." Louis soon learned to "take precautions" as he put it. He would eat his fill before calling the boys in for lunch.

The year 1914 drew slowly to a close. The great war in Europe grew in intensity as nation after nation took sides in the conflict. But in America, President Wilson vowed to keep the country out of the war. Domestic issues at home outweighed the news from distant war fronts. Henry Ford made headlines with his decision to pay workers a minimum of $5.00 per day—a hitherto unheard of wage for unskilled workers. Many people left New Orleans to join the rush to Detroit in search of prosperity and higher-paying jobs.

But young Louis Armstrong continued his rather humdrum life in New Orleans' Third Ward as the winter passed slowly and a fragrant, budding spring came once more to the Crescent City. He had grown to be a tall, sturdy young man as he approached his fifteenth birthday. He began longing once more for the old haunts and the hustle and bustle of Perdido. About this time, Louis' father and stepmother had another baby—a healthy little girl they named Gertrude after her mother. Now there were just too many mouths to feed on the meager incomes of Willie and his wife. Louis decided to return to Mayann and his stepfather, Gabe. He talked it over with both his parents, and one afternoon in the summer of 1915 he packed up his few belongings and walked back over to his old neighborhood.

Though Louis was welcomed into his father's home and was very busy managing the household while Willie and Gertrude worked, he soon began longing for the old haunts and hustle and bustle of Perdido Street. He decided to return to Mayann and his stepfather, and one day packed up his few belongings and walked back over to his old neighborhood (opposite).

That evening, Louis finished his supper and decided to take a walk along Perdido Street to see how many of the old gang he could find. One by one he found most of them—Cocaine Buddy Martin, Georgie Gray, and Redhead Happy and Little Mack from the old quartet. All were as happy to see Louis as he was to see them. They even sang a few of their old songs—just for old times' sake. All of them were a little older of course, more grown up, but generally the people and the neighborhood had changed little since that New Year's Eve so long ago.

Many of his pals had seen Louis the day he had marched up Perdido at the head of the Waifs' Brass Band. Louis beamed with pride as they told him how great he had looked in his uniform and how amazed they had been to hear him playing the cornet so well. He told them all about his days at the home and all about the people he had met there—especially Mr. Davis. He told them of all the different places he had played with the band and the marches he had made all around the city.

They recalled too, the forays the little quartet had made along Rampart Street, performing their routines for pennies. And they all howled in glee as Redhead Happy told of how frightened

the group had been when the detective caught Louis and hauled him off to jail on that New Year's Eve. Even Louis could find it hilarious now, but he freely admitted that he had been the most frightened boy in New Orleans at the time.

At last the group of old pals broke up for the evening and headed for home. As he trudged slowly along, Louis relived in his mind the many wonderful moments he had known while playing the cornet in the band. He grinned to himself as he remembered how upset Mr. Davis would be whenever Louis "took off" on a ragtime tune. Even as he remembered, the haunting wail of a cornet playing ragtime drifted along Perdido and echoed through the darkened alleys. Instinctively, Louis turned to find the source of these glorious tunes that filled the night air. Turning down a darkened alley, following the sound, Louis soon found himself at the rear of Funky Butt Hall.

Still too young to be allowed inside, Louis found an open window where he could look in and watch the dancers gyrating frantically to the syncopated rhythms of the band. As he peered through the blue haze of tobacco smoke, Louis could make out the form of the cornetist who strained and swayed as he blew clear and ringing ragtime notes through his horn. It was none other than the great Bunk Johnson himself.

As Louis watched, his fingers worked feverishly at the valves of an imaginary cornet. With each note Bunk Johnson blew, Louis tried to imagine the positions of the valves and he pursed his lips against the mouthpiece of his invisible horn. He watched each move Bunk Johnson made, and soon he was swaying and mocking every motion of the bandleader. At last the band took a breather, and Louis stood in the darkened alley perspiring from his own efforts. He watched as the crowd gathered around Johnson, showering him with praise and adulation. At that moment, Bunk Johnson became the most enviable man in the world to young Louis Armstrong.

Louis watched from his secret vantage point for some time and then, well past midnight, he trudged wearily home to bed. His dreams that night were of a huge ballroom filled with people who had come to hear the sweetest, most powerful tones ever blown through a cornet. There was a big band in his dream, whose members, beautifully attired in tuxedos, were playing a new style of blues and ragtime. But the bandleader was the star, and he thrilled

his audience with frequent soaring breaks and solos on the finest cornet in the world. The name of the leader was Louis Armstrong.

In the morning, Louis awoke to the realities of life in the Third Ward. Everyone else in the family was a breadwinner, each bringing home his or her share to help support the household. No one was making much more than a pittance, however, and Louis was anxious to find work so he could bring home his share. After the others had left for work, Louis went out to begin his search for employment.

Of course, his ambition was to play in a band for a living. But he had neither a cornet nor the money with which to buy one. Besides, none of the honky-tonk owners were likely to hire a boy of fifteen. His dreams of a musical career would have to wait. In the meantime, he would try to find just any kind of work.

After several days of fruitless searching, he finally took a job selling newspapers. He was back where he had been before being sent to the Waifs' Home. He had applied for work at Konowsky's Coal Company, but was told he was too big to be a helper and too young to handle the mules. All the encouragement and self-confidence he had acquired at the home were now dwindling in the face of the frustrations of idleness and poverty. The fifty cents or a dollar he would bring in each night after selling papers would not even pay for his share of the family's grocery bill.

Months passed, and Louis tried his hand at several jobs. Occasionally he found a day's work as a stevedore on the waterfront. This was back-breaking toil even for a grown man, and Louis would

One night Louis heard the haunting wail of a cornet playing ragtime. Instinctively following the sound, he soon found himself at the rear of Funky Butt Hall, where he saw an admiring crowd listening to the great cornetist, Bunk Johnson (second from left, back row), who immediately became the most enviable man in the world to the young boy.

47

arrive home at night so tired and bruised he could hardly get out of bed the next day. On one occasion he got a job unloading a banana boat. This meant slinging a huge stalk of bananas over his shoulder and carrying it off the boat to a waiting wagon. About mid-morning, as Louis bent low under a heavy load of bananas, he felt something scurry across his hand and down his back. Turning to see what it could be, he discovered a huge wharf rat darting across the dock. Louis had carried the rodent off the ship in his load of bananas. That was too much for him, and when he learned that there often were snakes concealed in the bananas he quit the job on the spot.

At last Louis found a steady job that paid a reasonable wage. Through the efforts of his stepfather, he was taken on as a coal-cart driver for the Andrews Coal Company. It was hard work, but Louis was growing bigger and stronger all the time.

"From seven in the morning to five in the evening I would haul hard coal at fifteen cents per load," he was to write later. "And I loved it. I felt like a real man when I shoveled a ton of coal into my wagon."

At last he was doing his share to provide for the family and often had a few cents left over to spend on himself. Now on Saturday nights he could attend the dances at Funky Butt Hall or Economy Hall and hear musicians like Bunk Johnson and King Oliver in person. On fine Sunday afternoons, he and his pals would go down to Lincoln Park and listen to the ragtime bands fill the air with their music. And every time Louis heard that music he ached to hold a cornet once again and blow some notes of his own.

Then one night in the summer of 1916, Louis was standing in Henry Matranga's honky-tonk waiting for the band to arrive. At last the drummer and guitarist entered and walked over to Matranga to tell him that the trumpeter would be unable to appear that night. "He's sick," they said.

The owner exploded in a rage. "How can I run a dance without a trumpet player?" he screamed. "Well, that fel-

low has played here for the last time. This happens once or twice a week lately and I'm going to find myself a new trumpet player!"

One of Louis' friends spoke up and asked, "Why don't you hire Satchmo here?"

"You play a trumpet?" the man asked.

"No," said Louis, "I play a cornet."

"Well," said Matranga, "Same thing. I'll take you on if you can start playing right away." This was the chance of a lifetime for Louis and he was eager to accept. But there was one matter he almost overlooked. He had no instrument!

"I'll fix that," said Matranga. "I'll buy a cornet and if you don't miss a single night for the next two months it'll be yours. Is that a deal?"

Louis could scarcely believe his ears. Doubts at once ran through his mind— he hadn't played a note in nearly two years. But he remembered Mr. Davis' parting words as he left the Waifs' Home. Besides, what did he have to lose?

"I'll take it," he finally answered with as much self-confidence as he could muster.

With that, the owner took Louis by the arm and led him down the street to a pawnshop. The pawnbroker had a cornet in the window and, after a little bargaining, Matranga bought the instrument.

Outside the shop, Matranga shoved the cornet at Louis and said, "Now get back to my place and play that thing."

Things had happened so fast that Louis had to pinch himself to find if it was all really true. It was true indeed, and at last he was getting the chance he had dreamed of for months. As it turned out, this was the second turning point in the musical career of Louis Armstrong. From that day forward, music and his cornet or trumpet would become a major part of his life.

Pausing under a streetlamp, Louis took out a clean white handkerchief and lovingly polished the gleaming instrument. Then, after planting a big kiss on the cornet, he hurried off to his first performance as a paid musician.

The First Steps With Destiny

In the small band at Matranga's there were only a pianist called Boogers, a drummer known as Goobee, and Louis with his newly acquired cornet. The trio made big music, however, and Louis blew until his lips were so sore he began to hit false notes. As they raced through number after number and the hours dragged by, Louis knew he needed some relief from his playing. With the piano and drums as accompaniment, he began to sing the blues and ragtime numbers he had performed with his quartet some four years before. Even at this early age there was a magnetism to the Louis Armstrong voice and the crowd that night at Matranga's stopped to listen.

After having shuddered at the bad notes Louis had hit on the cornet, the owner was somewhat relieved by his patrons' reaction to the boy's singing. Perhaps he hadn't made such a bad deal after all.

It was four in the morning when the last customer left the hall and the trio broke up and headed for home. Louis stopped by the cash register on the way out to collect his wages—fifteen cents. This was a very small amount even for a sixteen-year-old boy. But Louis knew he hadn't performed very well on the cornet that night. Matranga told him that if it hadn't been for his singing he would have fired the boy on the spot.

By 1916, Louis had a good job that paid a reasonable wage, and was doing his share to provide for the family. Now on Saturday nights he could attend the dances at Funky Butt Hall or Economy Hall and hear musicians like Bunk Johnson and Joe "King" Oliver in person. One night Louis was standing in Henry Matranga's honky-tonk waiting for the band to arrive. When the trumpeter failed to appear, one of Louis' friends suggested that Matranga hire Louis. He agreed to try the young boy, and this became the second turning point in the musical career of Louis Armstrong. From that day forward, music and his cornet or trumpet would become a major part of his life.

Louis didn't bother to alibi that he had not played a cornet in a year and a half. But he vowed to himself that he would devote much time to practice and eventually earn a bigger wage. At least he had, in effect, made his first installment on his instrument. In two months it would be his and by that time he would be making beautiful music with his horn.

He trudged wearily home, heartbroken at his performance but at the same time full of pride at being a paid musician. The quiet determination that was to mark the character of Louis Armstrong in his later years was already evident in the dog-tired teen-ager who tumbled into bed just as the sun began to rise over Lake Pontchartrain. This was only the beginning, he told himself. Some-day he would be in a class with Bunk Johnson and Joe Oliver.

It seemed as if he had barely drifted off to sleep when Mayann began shaking him. "Time to get up," she was saying. "Time to go for that old mule and coal wagon." Tired and bleary eyed, Louis told his mother of his new job at Ma-tranga's as he gulped down his break-fast. His sister, Mama Lucy, was scorn-ful.

"Fifteen cents for playing all night?" she sneered. "You must be crazy!"

Mayann, too, thought the long hours were hardly worth the small amount Louis brought home. But she knew her son had his heart set on being a musi-cian and she would not discourage him.

Despite his aching bones, Louis was jubilant as he delivered his loads of coal that morning. When lunchtime came, he raced for home instead of eating with his fellow drivers. Bounding up the stairs, he took his cornet from its shelf above his bed and sat down to practice. He practiced for a solid hour before wolfing down a quick sandwich and racing off to his mule and wagon.

This was to be his daily routine for several weeks, and soon he recaptured the skills he had acquired at the Waifs' Home. Gradually, his lips became con-

ditioned to the horn and he soon mastered the band's routines. Matranga was pleased at the progress Louis had made with his horn, but even happier that the boy's songs were so popular with the crowds. He insisted that Louis continue his singing. Presently Louis' wages were raised to $1.25 per night.

Louis' reputation spread throughout the area and the crowds at Matranga's increased as people flocked to hear the singing and playing of this new young man with a horn. Louis was a modest lad who preferred not to be in the spotlight. But fame, even though it was only local, thrust him into the public eye. He was now recognized wherever he went in the neighborhood as the featured entertainer at Matranga's. And he was rapidly becoming a polished performer.

One Saturday night, as Louis was blowing his cornet with extra power and force, in walked Joe "King" Oliver, who was playing trumpet for the famous Pete Lala. Louis, completely engrossed in his playing, did not notice Oliver, who sat quietly and listened as the band delivered a rocking rendition of "Panama." As the number ended and Louis told the band to "take five," Oliver walked up to the little bandstand.

"I've been wanting to hear you for some time, Dipper, "Oliver said. "They told me you were good and I wanted to see for myself. They were right."

Louis could scarcely believe his ears. These compliments were coming from the greatest trumpet player in the South. Perhaps all the hours he had spent playing his horn in this smoke-filled hall had been worth it. Louis mumbled his thanks and then listened respectfully as Joe offered a few pointers. Then Louis asked Oliver if he would care to "sit in" and play a number or two with the band.

Hearing this request, the crowd demonstrated its approval with cheers and applause and Oliver agreed to play. Louis followed King to the bandstand and stood in openmouthed admiration

as the great one filled the hall with the gorgeous full tones of a blues number. As the crowd urged Oliver on to number after number, Louis joined the group with his rich singing voice. That night at Matranga's was a night to remember. Those fortunate enough to have been there would tell of it for months to come.

Oliver took an immediate liking to Louis and that night marked the beginning of a friendship that was to last for many years. From that moment forward, the career of Louis Armstrong would be strongly influenced by the man who came to hear him play at Matranga's.

"Joe Oliver taught me more than anyone—he took up his time with me. If there is anybody who should get any credit . . . please give it to the great master of the olden days—Joseph 'King' Oliver," Louis was to say later. "Yass Lawd . . . There's the man that's responsible for my everything in the world of Swing-Jazz-Hot-Ragtime or any kind of music you might call it . . . Joe used to call himself my stepfather, because I was like a son to him, he said. He sure acted like a father to me."

It was now 1917 and America had joined the Allies in Europe. Louis registered for the draft, hoping the army might have a spot for a trumpeter or bugler. But weeks and months rolled by and he was not called. Then came another dip in his career.

In the fall of 1917, many of the honky-tonks in the Third Ward district were closed down on orders from the Secretary of War. Among those establishments forced to close their doors was Matranga's. Louis was out of work once more—along with about two hundred other musicians. Most of the star performers still found work.

Joe Oliver was playing with Kid Ory's band in the French Quarter. But Louis was forced to seek work driving a milk wagon. It seemed like the end of the world for the young cornet player as his dreams came crashing down around him.

Months dragged by and the only chance Louis had to play his cornet was at funerals. The tragic influenza epidemic of 1918 struck hard at the Third Ward, and for awhile there were several funerals daily. It was a sad and bitter year for the disheartened Louis.

Then on November 11, almost a year to the day since the honky-tonks were closed, peace came in Europe with the signing of the Armistice. As the nation began to return to normalcy, the honky-tonks reopened in New Orleans. Louis, who had changed from milk wagon back to coal wagon, immediately gave up that manual labor for the last time, dusted off his cornet, and went out in search of a job.

Many cabaret owners remembered Louis' reputation and he received offers to play short sessions at various places around the city. Then one day he was asked to form a group of his own and play for a week at a place called the Brick House in Gretna on the west side of the Mississippi. "In all my whole career, the Brick House was one of the toughest joints I ever played in," Louis would recall later. "It was the honky-tonk where levee workers would congregate every Saturday night. Those guys would drink and fight one another like circle saws. Bottles would come flying over the bandstand like crazy, and there was lots of just plain common shooting and cutting. But somehow all of that jive didn't faze me at all, I was so happy to have someplace to blow my horn."

One night at Matranga's, Joe "King" Oliver walked in and heard Louis play. Oliver took an immediate liking to Louis and that night marked the beginning of a friendship that was to last for many years. When Oliver left New Orleans for Chicago, he recommended Louis as his replacement on the cornet with Kid Ory's band. Ory (opposite) took the suggestion and offered the job, which Louis accepted immediately.

It was here that Louis fell in love for the first time with a pretty Creole girl named Daisy Parker. All the men had eyes for Daisy when she arrived, but it was Louis with whom Daisy fell in love. They were married soon, but it was to be a stormy relationship destined for failure.

Meanwhile, Joe Oliver and the great clarinetist Jimmy Noone had left New Orleans for Chicago, where dance-hall owners were crying for good jazz musicians. When he left Kid Ory's band, Oliver recommended Louis as his replacement on the cornet. Ory took Oliver's suggestion and offered the job, which Louis accepted immediately.

This became Louis' first musical association with many of the great men in jazz. Sidney Bechet played the clarinet and was later replaced by Johnny Dodds. Henry Morton played drums and Freddie Keppard played the guitar. All were among the greatest of the many New Orleans musicians who made jazz what it is today.

As for Louis, he was fast becoming recognized as the greatest cornet player in New Orleans. Always a hard-working performer, Louis was also a perfectionist. Despite his rapidly growing fame and popularity, he was constantly testing, improvising, and improving his style—a style that in later years many would try to copy but few would be able to master. Now, playing with some of the best jazz musicians in the country, Louis was able to develop further refinements of what was eventually recognized as the Armstrong style.

Louis was already demonstrating the power of a Buddy Bolden—but there was a difference. Louis held a masterful control of his power. The blasting force of his lungs barreled through his horn to emerge as rich, vibrant tones—every note clear and true.

"Even as a small kid I believed in finesse," Louis would write later. "That was the first thing Mr. Peter Davis taught me—out in the Colored Waifs' Home for Boys. 'Tone,' he said. 'A musician with tone can play any kind of music, whether it's classical or ragtime!' Bunk Johnson cut everybody for tone.

"Johnson had," Louis continued, "the most beautiful tone, the best imagination, and the softest sense of

The job in Kid Ory's band became Louis' first musical association with many of the great men in jazz, including clarinetists Johnny Dodds (opposite top) and Sidney Bechet (opposite bottom), and guitarist Freddie Keppard (opposite middle right). Clarinetist Jimmy Noone (opposite middle left) had left with Oliver for Chicago.

phrasing," of any trumpeter in New Orleans. There are many old-time jazz experts, however, who will say that Johnson's enthusiastic young admirer eventually surpassed both Bunk and King Oliver in all departments.

Louis was later to write that, "Oliver was the strongest and the most creative. And he had such range and such wonderful creations in his soul! He created some of the most famous phrases you hear today, and trends to work from."

There is no denying the greatness of Bolden, Oliver, or Johnson or the scope of their contributions to the art of jazz. But a deep sense of modesty prevents Louis from repeating what is often stated by jazz enthusiasts—that Louis "Satchmo" Armstrong is the greatest trumpet player of them all.

From the time he joined Kid Ory's band, Louis was in great demand throughout the clubs and cabarets of New Orleans. Occasionally he would sit in as a guest player with the Tuxedo Band, led by another famed jazz cornetist—the great Oscar Celestin. And often he made appearances at funeral processions along with the other great musicians of the day.

Then in the spring of 1919, Louis got an offer of a job with Fate Marable's Jaz-E-Saz Band, that played on the Mississippi River excursion boats.

"When he asked me to join his orchestra I jumped at the opportunity," Louis remembers. "It meant a great advancement in my musical career because his musicians had to read music perfectly. Ory's men did not."

Louis went on to explain his reasons for joining Marable. "I found out that Fate Marable had just as many jazz greats as Kid Ory, and they were better men besides because they could read music and they could improvise. Fate's

---

In the spring of 1919, Louis was offered a job with Fate Marable's Jaz-E-Saz Band, that played on the Mississippi River excursion boats. "When he asked me to join his orchestra I jumped at the opportunity," Louis remembers. "It meant a great advancement in my musical career because his musicians had to read music perfectly. Ory's men did not." In the photograph at left, two young boys watch the passing of one of the old Mississippi River sternwheelers, much like the one on which Louis Armstrong played.

In the year 1919, Louis Armstrong joined Fate Marable's band on the Mississippi River excursion boat Sydney. With smoke billowing from their tall stacks the river boats plied the lazy Mississippi between New Orleans and St. Louis, stopping at many small towns. At each town, the Sydney sold tickets for excursions on the river. As the passengers came aboard, Fate Marable would play on the boat's steam calliope. Then, as the boat turned out from the dock, the jazz band—with Louis on cornet—began to play the music that many of the passengers were hearing for the first time.

Besides spreading the gospel of New Orleans jazz, the band was incidently and quietly brushing aside the racial barriers that existed along the river. As Louis explained in his autobiography, "Fate Marable's Band deserves credit for breaking down a few barriers on the Mississippi—barriers set up by Jim Crow. We were the first colored band to play most of the towns at which we stopped, particularly the smaller ones . . . Before the evening was over they loved us."

The first summer spent away from his beloved New Orleans was a long one for Louis. For awhile there was new excitement just around the next bend of the river. New towns, new faces, new crowds, and the swinging beat of jazz, ragtime, blues, and Dixieland kept him from getting homesick. The vagabond life was grand.

By the time summer had waned, Louis began getting homesick for the familiar sights and sounds of his native city. At last the old steamboat pulled out into midstream and headed south, past the moss-draped bayous, to the city on the river's great crescent.

Just like the words of the song Basin Street Blues, they were indeed "steamin' down the river—down to New Orleans." Each chug of the engine and every turn of the great paddle wheel brought Louis closer and closer to his "land of dreams."

At last the river traffic began to increase; as the old steamboat glided gracefully around the great bend of the river the familiar docks came into sight. As the boat nudged gently into its berth, Louis searched for familiar faces.

At last he spotted his mother Mayann and his sister Mama Lucy. Louis stepped ashore for a happy reunion.

Another chapter in the life of Louis Armstrong was closed. He had sailed the length and breadth of the mighty "Missysip" and he had returned a more polished performer. There would be two more summers on the river, but these were only a prelude to the worldwide crusades Louis would make in the years ahead.

In Fate Marable's band on board the Sydney, Fate himself (above left) played the piano. A list of the other musicians playing the river boats sounds like a roll call of the jazz hall of fame. The great Johnny St. Cyr (above right) played the guitar. The most famous bass player of them all, Pops Foster, and drummer Baby Dodds (below right) rounded out the rhythm section. Baby Dodds' big brother Johnny played the clarinet, as did the one and only Alphonse Picou (below left), who Louis rates as the "finest clarinetist in New Orleans."

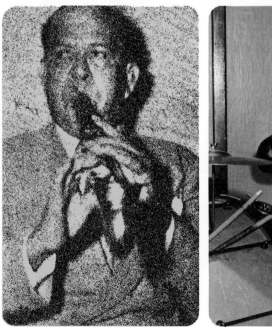

had a wide range and they played all the latest music because they could read at sight. Kid Ory's band could catch on to a tune quickly, and once they had it no one could outplay them. But I wanted to do more than fake the music all the time because there is more to music than just one style. I lost no time in joining the orchestra on the *Sydney*."

Louis stayed with the Marable band for three summer seasons and played on the other two boats of the line, the *Saint Paul* and the *J. S.* Once again, he had the opportunity to play with some of the finest musicians in the South. Marable paid good wages and demanded and got the best performers available.

Fate himself played the piano. A list of the other musicians playing the river boats sounds like a roll call of the jazz hall of fame. The great Johnny St. Cyr played guitar. The most famous bass player of them all, Pops Foster, and drummer Baby Dodds rounded out the rhythm section. Baby Dodds' big brother Johnny played the clarinet, as did the one and only Picou, who Louis rates as the "finest clarinetist in New Orleans." On a trip to Davenport, Iowa, where the boats were put up for the winter, Louis met the brilliant cornet player Bix Beiderbecke. Back in New Orleans, Louis stepped off the boat to meet Jack Teagarden, the trombonist, and began a friendship that was to last for nearly half a century.

It was an important three years for young Louis as he continued to perfect his style and develop his mastery of the cornet in association with the greatest names in jazz.

During the winter seasons he played in a variety of places, including Tom Anderson's Arlington Annex and the Orchard Cabaret in the French Quarter with Zutty Singleton's band. And there was a season at a place on Rampart Street called "The Real Thing."

Louis was in big demand and never lacked for a job—and he was receiving good wages. The steady diet of red beans and rice could be varied now, and Mayann turned out such fine dishes as Creole gumbo, fried chicken, and best of all Louis thought, her delicious jumbalaya. "It is a concoction of diced Bologna sausage, shrimp, oysters, and hard shell crabs mixed with rice and flavored with tomato sauce," Louis explains. "If you ever tasted Mayann's jumbalaya and did not lick your fingers my name is not Louis Satchmo Daniel Armstrong."

Louis had now reached the top in New Orleans. Life was good. He enjoyed a considerable measure of fame and popularity around the city and he had a steady income. Louis Armstrong was now twenty-two years old, however, and the fires of his ambition still burned brightly. He was anxious to move on to bigger and better things. He knew that, to realize his ambitions, he would have to leave his beloved New Orleans. But other musicians had left in years gone by only to return after a few months, broken in spirit and without funds. Louis felt a deep sense of responsibility to Mayann and Mama Lucy and was hesitant to take the gamble of moving to another city in search of work.

Then, in the summer of 1922, a telegram arrived from Joe "King" Oliver up in Chicago. Oliver now had a band of his own and was playing nightly at the Lincoln Gardens. "Come immediately," the telegram read, "Have job for you in my band." Once more the King himself was offering Louis a chance to move ahead in the field of jazz. Here at last was an opportunity to make a name for himself outside his home area.

"I would not risk leaving for anyone else," Louis remembers. "I had seen too many of my little pals leave home and come back in bad shape."

Louis packed his belongings, bade farewell to his family and friends, and left on the morning train for Chicago. And so began Louis Armstrong's final journey to stardom and a permanent niche in the annals of American jazz.

Jazz is King

Louis thought the long train ride to Chicago would never end. He bought a newspaper to take his mind off the anxieties he felt as he moved farther and farther away from his old hometown. There was little news of interest. President Harding was concerned about the wholesale price index of farm products. Men named Taylor and Young were working with a new invention called radar. On the sports page, an article mentioned that heavyweight champion Jack Dempsey might sign for a match with Harry Wills. In New York, Babe Ruth was in a hitting slump and it was a pretty sure thing he would not come near his record fifty-nine home runs of the previous season.

Louis put the paper aside and turned to watch the passing scenery outside the train window. Gradually the fields and farms turned to suburbs, and finally the towering buildings of the "Windy City" came into view.

Once on the station platform, Louis searched anxiously for Joe Oliver. A million faces seemed to pass him by, but there was no sign of "Papa Joe." At last Louis hailed a cab and told the driver to take him to Lincoln Gardens. When he arrived, he could hear the sound of Oliver's eloquent cornet echoing from the building even before he left the cab.

Pushing his way through the clapping, dancing crowd, Louis finally arrived at the bandstand just as the band took a break. Not only was King Oliver there but many of the old friends Louis had played with back in New Orleans. Baby Dodds and his big brother Johnny were there, along with Honore Dutrey and Bill Johnson, the great bass player. It was like old home week.

When the band resumed its playing, Louis stood by the stage and listened. "I started wondering if I could hold my own with such a fine band," Louis recalled later. But "Papa Joe" reassured him.

"Have a seat son; we're going to do our show. You might as well stick around and see what's happening because you start work tomorrow night."

That night, Oliver took Louis home to stay with his family. As he enjoyed the friendly atmosphere among good friends, Louis' old self-confidence returned. He was relaxed now and anxious only to start playing with the band.

The next afternoon Louis went over to the club to rehearse and met for the first time Oliver's pianist—a pretty young woman by the name of Lillian Hardin. She was a college graduate whose main musical interest was in the classical field. But she was a talented

---

In the summer of 1922, a telegram arrived from Joe "King" Oliver in Chicago. Oliver now had a band of his own and was playing nightly at the Lincoln Gardens. "Come immediately," the telegram read. "Have job for you in my band." Louis packed his belongings, bade farewell to his family and friends, and left on the morning train for Chicago. And so began his final journey to stardom and a permanent niche in the annals of American jazz. One of the first people he met in Chicago was Oliver's pianist, a pretty young woman named Lillian Hardin (opposite). "Lil" took an interest in Louis and concentrated on helping him learn to read music. The friendship grew, and in 1924, Louis and Lil were married.

and exciting jazz pianist—and she could read music better than anyone in the band.

Louis was to play second cornet to Oliver's lead. Though he had been a featured performer back in New Orleans, Louis felt he could still learn much from the man they called "King," and he was content to concentrate on the job he was hired to do.

"I had hit the big time," Louis wrote later. "I was up North with the greats. I was playing with my idol, the King, Joe Oliver. My boyhood dream had come true at last."

Gradually, Oliver allowed Louis to take more solos and soon the crowd was calling for more and more of the dynamic young cornetist. From the first evening, Louis' singing made a big hit with the audience. One of the favorites was his own composition, called "I Wish I Could Shimmy Like My Sister Kate."

Lil Hardin took a genuine interest in the young man. She recognized the greatness of his playing, though she knew it needed refinements. She concentrated on helping Louis learn to read music.

In March of 1923, just seven months after Louis joined the band, they made five recordings. On the last, a piece called "Chimes Blues," Louis made his first recorded solo. Later that year Oliver's band made several other recordings, including "Sobbin' Blues," "Canal Street Blues," "New Orleans Stomp," "High Society Rag," and many others. Though few could have realized it then, these records were to become classics—priceless collectors' items.

On February 5, 1924, Louis and Lil were married—an event that proved to be another turning point in the career of Satchmo Armstrong. Louis rented

Pictured at left are the 1933 members of King Oliver's Creole Jazz Band. From left to right, they are Johnny Dodds, clarinet; Warren "Baby" Dodds, drums; Honore Dutrey, trombone; Louis Armstrong, trumpet; Joe "King" Oliver, trumpet; Lil Hardin, piano; and Bill Johnson, banjo.

an apartment—the nicest he had ever lived in. The couple moved in along with Louis' mother Mayann, who had arrived unexpectedly from New Orleans after receiving word that Louis was sick. Louis was delighted to see his mother and, of course, she was relieved to find that the rumors were untrue. Louis persuaded her to stay on in Chicago with Lil and him.

Shortly after their marriage, Louis and Lil left the Oliver band to work at the Dreamland Cafe, where Louis became the featured cornetist. Lil had finally persuaded Louis that he should aspire to bigger things than second-cornet position. By now King Oliver also recognized the tremendous potential Louis had as an individual performer. Reluctantly, he bade Louis good-bye realizing, perhaps, that it should be Louis who bore the title of "King." It was evident by now that Louis had surpassed his old friend and idol on the instrument that had brought fame to them both.

Louis' stay at the Dreamland was brief. In October of 1924, he received a telegram from Fletcher Henderson in New York offering him a job at the Roseland Ballroom on Broadway. Here was an opportunity to play with a big orchestra that featured such greats as Coleman Hawkins, Buster Bailey, Big Charlie Green, Don Redman, and others. Mayann had already gone back to New Orleans and Lil was ready to pack up and make the journey east. Louis accepted the offer.

It was at this time that he switched from the cornet to the trumpet. The two instruments are similar, with the trumpet having a slightly higher range. The cornet, which all but disappeared with the advent of the swing bands, is generally considered to be capable of sweeter tones than the slightly larger trumpet.

It was with "Smack" Henderson that Louis completed his education in reading music. Smack was an arranger who scored his own music and, of course, his musicians were required to follow the score. Louis was thankful for the hours he had spent learning to read music, first under Peter Davis at the Waifs' Home, and then under Fate Marable on the river boats, and finally under the patient and watchful eye of Lil. He was to learn much more about sight-reading from Henderson.

The year and a half that Louis was with the Henderson band is sometimes referred to as "Fletcher's Louis Armstrong Period." Many jazz experts feel it was the greatest era in the illustrious career of Smack Henderson. Nearly forty records were cut during this period, most of which are collectors' items today. Louis is featured on three of the best—"Sugar Foot Stomp," "What-Cha-Call-Em Blues," and "Money Blues." On several other fine recordings, he accompanied the great blues singers Bessie Smith and Ma Rainey.

Late in 1925, Louis returned to Chicago to take his place in a band Lil had formed. At first the band was called Lil's Hot Shots, but it later came to be known as Louis Armstrong's Hot Five. Once again Louis was back with his old pals from New Orleans. Kid Ory was in the band, along with Johnny Dodds and Johnny St. Cyr. Lil and Louis rounded out the quintet that made jazz history for the next two years. The Hot Five briefly became the Hot Seven, with the addition of Baby Dodds on drums and Pete Briggs on tuba. Later it became a quintet once again and featured two all-time greats—Earl "Fatha" Hines and Zutty Singleton.

In 1924, Louis joined Fletcher Henderson's band at the Roseland Ballroom on Broadway in New York. During the time he was there, nearly forty records were cut by the band, most of which are collectors' items today. On several recordings, Louis accompanied the great blues singers Bessie Smith (opposite) and Ma Rainey.

d Muggsy

from

is Armstrong

Jazz critic Rudi Blesh has called this period of Louis' career his "four golden years." Besides playing with his Hot Five and Seven groups, Louis played frequently at the Vendome Theater with a large orchestra under the direction of Erskine Tate. There were also side trips to other clubs and other cities—even back to New York for a weekend at the Savoy. Louis was riding the crest of a wave of popularity such as he had never dreamed possible.

Then came the worst tragedy of his life. Word came up from New Orleans that Mayann was ill—very ill. Lil went to bring the aging lady to Chicago. No sooner had they arrived than Louis had his mother taken to a hospital. The doctors advised him that there was nothing they could do for Mayann.

Every day, Louis spent a little while at his mother's bedside. He saw to it that she got the finest care available, and he continued to hope and pray for a miracle. But the miracle never came, and one day Mayann quietly passed away. Louis was heartbroken, and later admitted that it was the only time in his adult life that he had cried. They laid Mayann to rest in Chicago's Lincoln Cemetery.

In the spring of 1926, Louis met Joe Glaser, who then owned the Sunset Cafe where Louis went to play with Carroll Dickerson's band. Though neither could have realized it then, this meeting was to be the start of one of the closest and most famous relationships in show business. Louis stayed at the Sunset until 1927, when he left on an ill-fated attempt to run his own busi-

Late in 1925, Louis returned to Chicago to take his place in a band Lil had formed. At first the band was called Lil's Hot Shots, but it later came to be known as Louis Armstrong's Hot Five. Members of the group, from left to right, were Armstrong, trumpet; Johnny St. Cyr, guitar; Johnny Dodds, clarinet; Kid Ory, trombone, and Lil Hardin, piano.

IN PERSON
LOUIS
ARMSTRONG
& ORCHESTRA
VAUDEVILLE
LOEW'S STATE
FREDRIC MARCH
"THE BUCCANEER"
FRANCISKA GAAL
LOUIS ARMSTRONG ORCH

ness in association with his pals Earl Hines and Zutty Singleton. The venture was short-lived and Louis ended up playing in Dickerson's band once again—this time at the Savoy.

When the contract at the Savoy had expired, a group of the bandsmen decided to stay together and form a new band with Louis as their leader. Deciding that New York offered the best prospects for employment, they formed a car caravan and headed east. They arrived in New York City at the same time the stock market crashed in 1929. With businesses failing by the dozen, things looked rather bleak. But Louis Armstrong was a magical name, and the group soon found employment at a theater in the Bronx. Shortly thereafter, they got a break and moved to the famous Connie's Inn in Harlem. Despite the depression now sweeping the country, Louis Armstrong and his band were riding high.

It was about this time that Louis' marriage began to break up. He and Lil finally decided to separate. Eventually they were divorced, but though they could not make a harmonious marriage, they had made a lasting mark together in the world of jazz.

At this time, jazz did not have the public acceptance it has today. Many Americans living beyond those particular neighborhoods where jazz flourished tended to consider the music undesirable. Thus, Louis and his associates were well known mainly to jazz enthusiasts. It was during his engagement at Connie's Inn that Louis got a break that resulted in his acceptance by the general public.

The break came in the form of an offer to play in a Broadway revue entitled *Hot Chocolates*. It was also to mark another turning point in the career of Louis Armstrong. For the first time, the name Louis Armstrong was up in lights along the "Great White Way." Fats Waller had written a song that Louis was to sing. His performances of that song were to make his name well known to countless millions of new fans. The song was "Ain't Misbehavin'."

Though many top entertainers have sung and recorded it since, Louis Armstrong's rendition is the one most in demand. The great success of that song led Louis gradually away from the pure jazz, Dixieland, and blues of his early years. During 1930, he began fronting for large orchestras and devoted more and more interest and effort to popular songs. It was a gradual turning, but a new era in the career of Louis Armstrong was beginning to develop. By the end of the decade, with the depression nearly over and the world teetering on the brink of global war, Louis was a recognized stage and show personality in his own right.

By the time the thirties ended, the name Louis Armstrong enjoyed international fame. And then it was not only jazz enthusiasts and blues lovers who spoke their praises of Satchmo. Millions of moviegoers and record collectors the world over recognized at a glance the wide smile, the dancing eyes, and the gravelly, rumbling voice of Louis Armstrong.

The world harkened to the songs and playing of the boy from Perdido Street.

In 1929, Louis got a break that resulted in his acceptance by the general public. Up to this time, Louis and his associates were well known mainly to jazz enthusiasts. The break came in the form of an offer to play in a Broadway revue entitled Hot Chocolates. *For the first time, the name Louis Armstrong was up in lights along the "Great White Way." By the time the 1930's ended, the name Louis Armstrong enjoyed international fame. Millions of people the world over recognized at a glance the wide smile, the dancing eyes, and the gravelly voice of Louis Armstrong.*

Return to New Orleans

There are many jazz enthusiasts who claim that Louis reached his peak as a pure jazz artist during the late twenties. As the thirties began, he shifted gradually to popular music and helped pave the way for the "swing" era of the big bands. But for the first half of the decade he traveled extensively, carrying with him the exciting music of jazz.

Following his engagement at Connie's Inn, he left for the West Coast and performed for nearly a year with Eddie Elkin's band at the Cotton Club in Culver City, a suburb of Los Angeles. It was here that he met for the first time "a little kid, a seventeen-year-old cat named Lionel Hampton, on drums." The boy was to go on to fame and fortune with bands of his own and earn a place in the history of jazz.

During Louis' tour in California, he made his first appearance in movies. These few short film features were only the first of many he would appear in over the coming years.

In 1931, Louis returned for a brief engagement at the Regal Theater in Chicago where he was welcomed back with open arms. He played to a capacity house every night as he entertained in his own inimitable style with such tunes as "Sleepy Time Down South," "Them There Eyes," and "You Rascal You." As a change of pace, Louis would swing lightly into such tender strains as "Georgia on My Mind," and then race off on a wild, screaming rendition of "Tiger Rag" or "Muskrat Ramble." As the crowds roared their approval, Louis reflected that it was nice to be back in "that toddlin' town"—Chicago.

But another city was calling Louis. That city on a great crescent bend of the Mississippi where magnolias bloomed and jazz was king. New Orleans beckoned, and after being away for nine years, Louis succumbed to homesickness. He longed for the sights and sounds of Perdido Street. His manager, Johnny Collins, arranged an engagement in Louis' hometown.

A date was set for Louis to appear at the Suburban Gardens with a band he had assembled in Chicago. Word

During the 1930's, Louis "Satchmo" Armstrong gradually shifted from pure jazz artist to a player of popular music, helping to pave the way for the "swing" era of the big bands.

spread like wildfire through the Third Ward: "Louis is coming home!" When Louis' train arrived at the station there were eight bands waiting to greet him. More than ten thousand persons screamed their welcome when he appeared on the platform. As Louis moved forward through the crowd, he suddenly found himself smothered in the embrace of his sister, Mama Lucy.

An open car was waiting to carry him on a triumphal ride back to his old district. As thousands of cheering spectators lined the streets, Louis waved from the slowly moving car and searched happily for familiar faces in the crowd. Occasionally an old friend would push through the crowd and trot alongside the car as Louis reached joyfully out to catch his hand.

The car came to a halt for a few moments, and Louis found himself looking at an old familiar banner that brought tears to his eyes. It read "Waifs' Home Colored Band." Then suddenly he was shaking hands with the home's director, Mr. Jones, and the entire staff. Mr. Davis came up to the car, too deeply moved to speak. But his eyes reflected the pride he felt for his former student.

Then Mr. Davis turned and gestured toward the little band, drawn up proudly in their uniforms. "They are walking in your footsteps, Louis. You are their hero and inspiration. Will you come out and see us while you're here?"

Louis grinned and waved to the wide-eyed youngsters and said to Mr. Davis, "I wouldn't miss that chance for all the world!"

Then the parade began to move once more, and soon the familiar sights of his boyhood haunts came into view. As they passed James Alley, Louis caught a glimpse of the old Chinaball tree he had climbed as a tot. Matranga's was gone and a church now stood on the site of old Funky Butt Hall. The Fisk School was still there, and the Parish Prison, and many other landmarks that Louis remembered with nostalgia. At last they arrived at the Astoria Hotel where the band was to stay. Louis was carried into the lobby, where he was able to escape to his room for a joyous reunion with Mama Lucy.

The next day, Louis kept his promise to visit the Waifs' Home. It had been exactly seventeen years since he had left. A program had been prepared in which all the boys and the staff participated. Louis, who had received acclaim and honors from all over the country, was thrilled and overwhelmed by the ceremony. His heart went out in appreciation to the eager and awestruck youngsters who did their very best to give him a fitting welcome.

One of the boys came shyly forward during the ceremony to hand Louis an old cornet. At first Louis was puzzled, and then he noticed something odd about the mouthpiece. The realization hit him—they were the file marks he had put there so many years ago as he reshaped the mouthpiece to fit his lips. While the whole school waited in anticipation, Louis fondled the little cornet and then put it to his lips and blew the sweetest notes that had ever come through the old horn. The great talent

By 1931, Louis succumbed to homesickness. New Orleans beckoned, and his manager arranged an engagement at the Suburban Gardens with a band that had been assembled in Chicago. Word spread like wildfire through the Third Ward that Louis was coming home, and more than ten thousand persons screamed their welcome when he appeared on the train platform. An open car carried him on a triumphal ride back to his old district as thousands of cheering spectators lined the streets. Among those who welcomed him home were Mr. Davis and the Waifs' Home Colored Band.

Mr. Davis had spoken of so long ago had returned, more gloriously developed than even he had dreamed possible.

Louis had supper with the boys that evening—red beans and gumbo—and then as twilight fell he walked slowly out to his automobile. For a few moments he paused and looked back at the little school as he considered all that had transpired in his life since he had last walked this way with his father.

In a sense, Louis and his music had grown up together in the years following his departure from the Waifs' Home. More than any other single musician, Louis Armstrong had developed jazz into the unique and dynamic force it had become by 1931. From the old Dixieland and blues tradition, Louis' masterful improvising had sparked the evolution of new patterns and rhythms that gave a name to the decade—the "Jazz Era." He, more than any other, had made jazz great. And he derived his own greatness from the music he did so much to develop. The destiny of Louis Armstrong, almost from the very beginning, had been inextricably interwoven with the destiny of jazz.

Many exponents of jazz have claimed that "pure jazz" began to fade in the early thirties—about the time Louis began playing more popular numbers. But jazz has been a changing thing with many branches shooting off from the main stem that flourished in the twenties. The music, which nevertheless remains strictly American, has taken many forms and many names. In the mid-thirties, "swing" evolved with the era of the big bands. Later there came "boogie woogie," "bop," "cool jazz," and "progressive jazz." Most people will agree that these are no more than

variations—though some are extreme—of the basic jazz concept.

To Louis, the subject was a matter of semantics. He once discussed the distinction between the names "jazz" and "swing."

"To me, as far as I could see it all my life, jazz and swing were the same thing. In the good old days of Buddy Bolden, in his days way back in nineteen hundred, it was called ragtime music. Later on in the years it was called jazz music, hot music, gutbucket, and now they've poured a little gravy over it and called it swing music. No matter how you slice it, it's still the same music. If anybody wants to know, a solo can be swung on any tune and you can call it jazz or swing."

Louis stayed in New Orleans until early 1932—the year Franklin Delano Roosevelt rode to the White House to the tune of "Happy Days Are Here Again." Then, after a brief stint in California, he made his first trip abroad.

In England, where he played at London's famed Palladium, Louis and his music were a smashing success. The English were ecstatic over the new music Louis had brought from America. In a wild demonstration of acclaim and approval they gave him standing ovations night after night and refused to let him leave the stage. He was frequently called back for several encores and he was presented with a handsome gold trumpet as a token of English admiration.

Louis returned to England the following year with his third wife, Alpha, and then went on to tour the capitals of Europe. Stockholm, Oslo, Copenhagen, Paris, Rotterdam, and Geneva all fell before the feet of the American who

captured the hearts of Europeans wherever he went. Only Germany refused him entry. Hitler was in power and jazz was blacklisted as a non-Aryan vice.

Louis stayed in Europe for about eighteen months on this occasion, finally succumbing to homesickness. Once back in the United States, Louis joined Luis Russell's orchestra, which eventually took his name. His association with this group was to last for over a decade.

It was at this time that Louis began another relationship that was to last until the present day. It is an association that is a rarity in the entertainment world where loyalties often fade under the pressures and demands of show business. In 1935, Joe Glaser, the owner of the Sunset Cafe in Chicago where Louis had worked in 1926 and 1927, became Louis' manager. Joe, or "Pops" as Louis calls him, has been more than a manager to Satchmo—he has been almost a father or big brother.

When "Pops" took over the reins of Louis' career, he gave up all his other business to devote full time to Louis. It was under Glaser's tutelage that Louis developed into the great entertainer that he is today. Louis respects and admires Glaser and the two are the closest of friends. "I can confide in him," Louis says. "I can trust him."

In 1936, Louis starred in his first full-length movie, called *Pennies From Heaven*, with Bing Crosby. This led to other film roles through the years, including *Every Day's a Holiday*, *Cabin in the Sky*, *The Glenn Miller Story*, and *High Society*. Louis also appeared in a play called *Swingin' the Dream* in 1939.

Louis' popularity has never waned since he reached the top back in the early thirties. In 1943, long after many

During the thirties, Louis had
roles in several movies, among
which were Going Places (left),
Cabin in the Sky, The Glenn
Miller Story, High Society, and
New Orleans (opposite, top).
Louis also appeared in a play
called Swingin' the Dream
(opposite, bottom) in 1939.

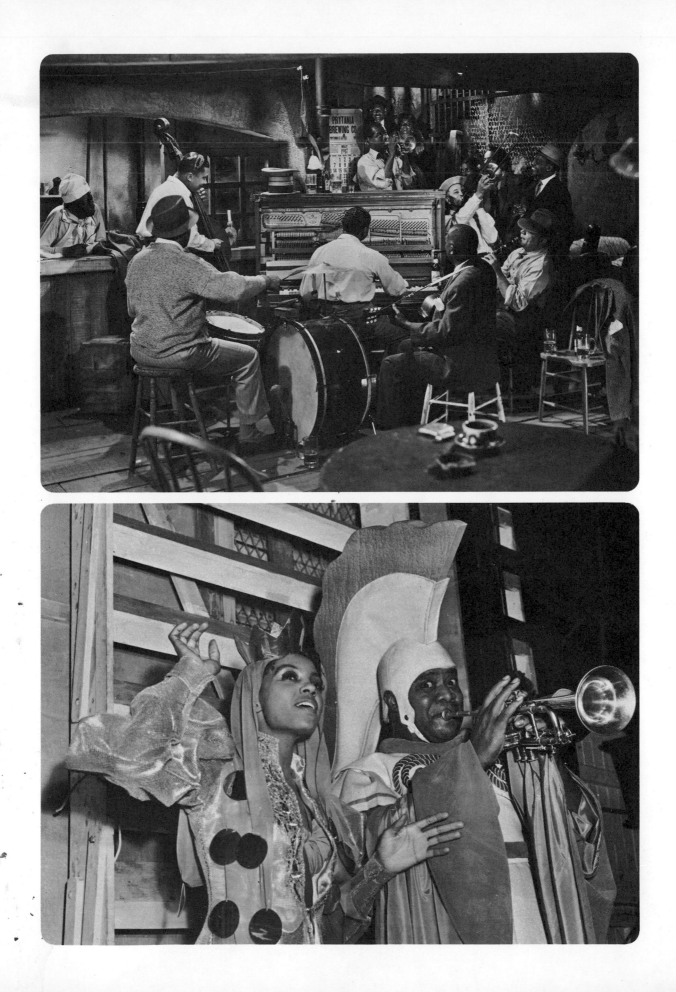

Carnival week in New Orleans was ending. That, of course, meant that Mardi Gras, the most festive day of all, had at last arrived. Literally "Fat Tuesday," it is the last day before Lent and caps a week of parades, balls, and fun seeking.

Throngs massed in the city streets, drinking, laughing, dancing, and cheering for just about anything. Carnival colors of purple, green, and gold were everywhere. Everyone anxiously awaited the appearance of Rex, King of the Carnival, who was to start the parade. He would soon step ashore from a yacht to ride an exotic float up St. Charles Avenue leading a procession that would stretch for more than thirty-five blocks.

Across the city, King Zulu stepped ashore from his barge at the New Basin Canal. A good natured spoof of King Rex, King Zulu mounted a gaudy float for a meandering ride throughout the city streets.

King Zulu first became a part of Mardi Gras in 1910. Because the white king Rex was supposed to have come from a faraway land, the Negroes decided their king would come to New Orleans from Africa. And so he has come every year since.

King Zulu for the year 1949, Louis "Satchmo" Armstrong, sat proudly on his float in his regal costume complete with a tinsel crown. Followed by blaring brass bands, Louis waved and bowed to the cheering crowds.

Hour after hour, the king and his cortége led his followers on a merry jaunt through the city streets. At last as dawn began to streak the sky, the reign of King Louis came to an exhausting but happy end. It had been one of the most memorable, fun-filled days of his life. Among all the honors Louis Armstrong had won as the greatest jazz trumpeter in the world, none came closer to his heart than that of being selected King of the Zulus. He has often said, "It had been my life-long dream to be the King of the Zulus, as it was the dream of every kid in my neighborhood. I finally got my wish . . . and I can hardly wait for the chance to be it again."

jazz "purists" claim he abandoned "virtuoso jazz," Louis won the first *Esquire* magazine jazz poll. He captured the honors in both the trumpet and vocal categories. In January of 1944 he was featured at the first jazz concert ever held in the Metropolitan Opera House and went on to win the magazine's poll again in 1945, 1946, and 1947.

In 1942, Louis—having divorced Alpha—married Lucille Wilson, his present wife, and when Louis is not on the road they live quietly in a modest home in Queens, New York.

In the years following World War II, Louis was much in demand in foreign countries where American GI's had introduced jazz and big-band swing. He has become a roving, globe-trotting ambassador of good will for his country. He toured Africa in 1956 and again in 1960 on a cultural mission for the United States Information Agency. In 1965 he made two excursions to Europe where he performed in many cities in the Iron Curtain countries. He is often referred to as the "Diplomat With a Horn."

The public affection for Louis Armstrong seems to grow with each passing year. Honors of all kinds are continually heaped upon the modest and unassuming man with the wide grin. In December of 1965, Carnegie Hall was jammed with his admirers as the American Guild of Variety Artists saluted his half-century in show business.

In the years following World War II, Louis was much in demand in foreign countries where American GI's had introduced jazz and big-band swing. He has become a roving, globe-trotting ambassador of good will for his country. On the opposite page he is shown (top) with his present wife, Lucille, at the entrance of the papal residence at Castel Gondolfo near Rome following their audience with Pope Pius XII in 1949. Swiss Guards flank the group. In 1959, he and his wife returned to Italy, and are shown here (opposite, bottom) near the ruins of the Colosseum in Rome. At right, top to bottom, Louis is shown on goodwill tours in Scotland, Switzerland, and West Germany.

On these pages, Louis is shown on tours of Africa. In the picture at the top of page 86, Lucille Armstrong and two chiefs of Ghana swing to Satchmo's brand of wonderful music during his 1957 goodwill tour of Europe and Africa. In 1960, Louis is greeted by a tribal chief on the trumpeter's arrival in Leopoldville, Congo (opposite, bottom). On the same trip, he is carried into a sports stadium in Leopoldville by native tribal dancers (right).

And Louis continues to astound the world with his amazing series of recording successes. In 1964, his recording of "Hello, Dolly!" sold over two million copies. It now ranks with his great rendition of "Blueberry Hill," made back in the thirties. His warm and guttural singing voice is probably the most imitated voice in the world.

Louis Armstrong began his musical career by dancing and singing for pennies on the streets of New Orleans. In the twilight of his career he remains one of the best-loved entertainers in the world. But his destiny lay in his mastery of jazz as expressed and phrased on a cornet or trumpet. The great pianist and jazz authority, Teddy Wilson, summed up Louis Armstrong's greatness in an interview in *Down Beat* magazine.

"I think Louis is the greatest jazz musician that's ever been. He had a combination of all the factors that make a good musician. He had balance . . . this most of all. Tone. Harmonic sense. Excitement. Technical skill. Originality. Every musician, no matter how good, usually has something out of balance, be it tone, too much imitativeness, or whatever. But in Armstrong everything was in balance. He had no weak point.

"I don't think there has been a musician since Armstrong who has had all the factors in balance, all the factors equally developed. Such a balance was the essential thing about Beethoven, I think, and Armstrong, like Beethoven, had this high development of balance. Lyricism, Delicacy. Emotional outburst. Rhythm. Complete mastery of his horn."

"OOOHHH YEEAAHHH!"

Louis Armstrong continues to astound the world with his amazing series of recording successes. In 1964, his recording of "Hello, Dolly!" sold over two million copies. At right he is shown with Carol Channing, star of the Broadway musical.

Summary

Louis Daniel "Satchmo" Armstrong and his music were born during the same time in the Negro district of New Orleans. They grew up together in the streets and alleys and honky-tonks "Back O' Town." They reached maturity together in Chicago and New York and together they gave a name to an epoch in American history—the "Jazz Era."

Both the man and the music had many adversities to overcome. The music was, for many years, rejected by the general public. Played almost exclusively in honky-tonks, cabarets, and speakeasies, by generally untutored musicians, it seemed destined for a minor role in the musical culture of America. It awaited the golden touch of a dynamic master musician who could crack the barriers of public opinion.

For Louis Armstrong, his walk with destiny led along a hard road filled with pitfalls and obstacles. He found a dream amid the squalor and deprivation of life in New Orleans' Third Ward where he was born. Sent to a correctional institution for boys at the early age of twelve, he emerged, not with a contempt or hate for society, but with new strength and determination to reach his goal. In an environment where the temptations of sin and crime were made more alluring by the prevailing poverty, he clung steadfastly to his principles and his dream.

From his very first contact with a musical instrument, Louis Armstrong displayed a natural and gifted talent. Those who recognized this latent potential offered advice and encouragement, but the development of the "Armstrong styling" derived from his own determination and natural sense of rhythm and tone. The warmth and beauty of his style, his phenomenal range, and his improvisations were great factors in winning the public to this purely American art form.

As the jazz era gave way to the "Swing Era" Louis concentrated more and more on popular music. From supreme jazz soloist he became one of show business's most-popular personalities. His fame soon spread abroad and he made frequent journeys to the far corners of the globe as a symbol of American jazz.

Today, "Satchmo" is one of the best-loved entertainers in America. And as a representative of America, he has won the affection of millions of people all around the world.

His walk with destiny has led from the lowest slums to the highest pinnacles of public acclaim. But his true destiny lay in his masterful interpretation of jazz. More than any other single individual, Louis Armstrong made jazz great. And in the process, Louis Armstrong achieved greatness.

Bibliography

"Akwaala, Satchmo." *Time*, November 9, 1959.

ALLEN, WALTER C. and BRIAN A. L. RUST. *King Joe Oliver*. Belleville, New Jersey: Allen & Rust, 1955.

ARMSTRONG, LOUIS. "Daddy How This Country Has Changed." *Ebony*, May, 1961.

———. *Satchmo—My Life in New Orleans*. New York: Prentice-Hall, 1954.

———. *Swing That Music*. New York: Longmans, Green, 1936.

ASBURY, HERBERT. *The French Quarter*. New York: Alfred A. Knopf, 1936.

BALLIETT, WHITNEY. *The Sound of Surprise*. New York: E. P. Dutton, 1959.

"Basin Street, Berlin." *Newsweek*, February 23, 1959.

BURLIN, NATALIE. *Songs and Tales from the Dark Continent*. New York: Schirmer, 1920.

CARMICHAEL, HOAGY. *The Stardust Road*. New York: Rinehart, 1946.

CONDON, EDDIE and RICHARD GEHMAN, eds. *Eddie Condon's Treasury of Jazz*. New York: Dial, 1956.

"Diplomat With a Horn." *Newsweek*, December 19, 1960.

EATON, JEANETTE. *Trumpeter's Tale: The Story of Young Louis Armstrong*. New York: Morrow, 1955.

FEATHER, LEONARD. *The Encyclopedia of Jazz*. New York: Horizon Press, 1955.

FINKLESTEIN, SIDNEY. *Jazz: A People's Music*. New York: Citadel, 1948.

GROSSMAN, WILLIAM L. and JACK W. FARRELL. *The Heart of Jazz*. New York: New York University Press, 1955.

HARRIS, REX. *Jazz*. New York: Grosset & Dunlap, 1955.

HUGHES, LANGSTON. *Famous Negro Music Makers*. New York: Dodd, Mead, 1961.

———. *The First Book of Jazz*. New York: Watts, 1955.

"Jazz." *Grolier Universal Encyclopedia*, Vol. 6, 1965.

JONES, MAX, ed. *Jazz Photo Album*. London: British Yearbooks, 1947.

KEEPNEWS, ORRIN and BILL GRAUER. *A Pictorial History of Jazz*. New York: Crown, 1955.

"Louis Armstrong." *Current Biography*, May, 1966.

"Louis Armstrong." New York *Herald Tribune*, June 18, 1961.

"Louis Armstrong." New York *Times Magazine*, November 20, 1960.

"Louis Armstrong." Toronto *Globe and Mail*, November 11, 1961 and August 7, 1965.

"Louis Armstrong." Washington *Post*, August 30, 1964.

"Louis Armstrong." *Who's Who in America*, 1964–65.

"Louis Armstrong Issue." *Record Changer*, July-August, 1950.

McCARTHY, ALBERT. *Louis Armstrong*. London: Cassell, 1960. (This book contains a good Armstrong Discography, pp. 81-87.)

———. *The Trumpet in Jazz*. London: The Citizen Press, 1945.

MERRIAM, ALAN P. *A Bibliography of Jazz*. Philadelphia: American Folklore Society, 1954.

MERYMAN, R. "Authentic American Genius." *Life*, April 15, 1966.

MILLSTEIN, GILBERT. "Africa Harks to Satch's Horn." New York *Times Magazine*, November 20, 1960.

RAMSEY, FREDERIC, JR. and C. E. SMITH, ed. *Jazzmen*. New York: Harcourt, Brace & World, 1939.

ROURKE, CONSTANCE. *American Humor*. New York: Harcourt, Brace, 1931.

SANDERS, C. L. "Louis Armstrong, The Reluctant Millionaire." *Ebony*, November, 1964.

"Satchmo Returns to his Home Town, Briefly." *New Republic*, November 13, 1965.

"Satchmo Goes Home." *Newsweek*, November 8, 1965.

SARGEANT, WINTHROP. *Jazz: Hot and Hybrid*. New York: Dutton, 1946.

SHAPIRO, NAT and NAT HENTOFF, eds. *Hear Me Talkin' to Ya*. New York: Rinehart, 1955.

SPAETH, SIGMUND. *A History of Popular Music in America*. New York: Random House, 1948.

STEARNS, MARSHALL. *The Story of Jazz*. New York: Oxford University Press, 1956.

TALLANT, ROBERT. *Voodoo in New Orleans*. New York: Macmillan, 1946.

"That Man on Trumpet." *Newsweek*, July 6, 1959.

"Up Among the Beatles." *Newsweek*, April 27, 1964.

WILLIAMS, M. "Armstrong Before Dolly." *Saturday Review*, October 17, 1964.

———. "Louis Armstrong and Jazz Rhythm." *American Record Guide*, November, 1962.

WORK, JOHN. *American Negro Songs*. New York: Howell, Soskin, 1940.

Index

Acknowledgments: Photographs on pages 2, 11, 13 (right), 14, 15, 20, 54, 58, 81 (bottom), 84, 85, 86, 87, and 89 from the files of Wide World Photos, Inc.; photographs on pages 8-9, 12, 64, 74, 80, and 81 (top) courtesy of Down Beat *magazine; photographs on pages 13 (left), 38, and 90 courtesy of Jack Bradley; photographs on pages 23, 30, 46-47, and 70-71 courtesy of Frederic Ramsey, Jr./Jazzmen; photographs on pages 57, 62 (top and bottom right), 66-67, and 68 courtesy of George Hoefer; photographs on pages 34-35, 62 (bottom left), and 72 courtesy of Orrin Keepnews and Jane Grauer. Illustrations on pages 17, 21, 24-25, 27, 28, 32, 37, 41, 42, 44, 49, 50-51, 53, 60-61, 76-77, 79, and 82-83 by Bob Brunton, Hollis Associates; illustrations on page 18 by John Hollis.*

Date Due			
JAN 23			
DEC 17			
APR 8			
APR 2			
OCT 20			
DEC 1			
MAR 26 1996			

G2
A

3718

Richards, Kenneth G
People of destiny:
Louis Armstrong